Isaac Bashevis Singer

Writings on Yiddish and Yiddishkayt

Isaac Bashevis Singer

Writings on Yiddish and Yiddishkayt
The War Years, 1939-1945

TRANSLATED AND EDITED BY DAVID STROMBERG

Isaac Bashevis Singer Writings on Yiddish and Yiddishkayt: The War Years, 1939-1945
Translated and edited by David Stromberg

White Goat Press, the Yiddish Book Center's imprint
Yiddish Book Center
Amherst, MA 01002
whitegoatpress.org

Printed in the United States of America at The Studley Press,
Dalton, MA
10 9 8 7 6 5 4 3 2 1

Paperback ISBN 979-8-9877078-9-0
Hardcover ISBN 979-8-9886773-0-7
Ebook ISBN 979-8-9886773-1-4

Library of Congress Control Number: 2023916083

Book and cover design by Michael Grinley

This book has been made possible with generous support from Robert L. Friedman

To the Jews of the Holocaust—
those who were murdered and those who survived

Table of Contents

Singer's Wartime Writings

There has always been a gap between the English-language author Isaac Bashevis Singer and the Yiddish writer who published under at least three pseudonyms: Yitskhok Bashevis, Yitskhok Varshavski, and D. Segal. This volume—selected from Singer's writings on Yiddish culture and Jewish life that first appeared in the *Forverts* from 1939 to 1945—is the first major effort to begin filling that gap. While the average Yiddish reader of the *Forverts* may not have known during this time period that Yitskhok Varshavski, under whose byline most of these articles appeared, was Yitskhok Bashevis—the younger brother of Yiddish writers Esther Kreitman and Israel Joshua Singer—it is possible to imagine that same reader wondering about the identity of this "Isaac from Warsaw." Whoever he was, he had a lot of opinions about the situation of the Jews in both Europe and the United States, before and during World War II, as well as the future of Jewish life in America. He was an unknown entity, but anyone reading his work could tell that he was deeply invested in his topic.

The writing collected in this volume, the first of three, covers the period between Singer's first appearance as Yitskhok Varshavski in the *Forverts* in April 1939, just months before the outbreak of World War II, and the end of 1945, when the war ended and Singer started serially publishing the Yiddish original of *The Fam-*

ily Moskat—his first major literary memorial to the life of Jews in Poland. During those years, his own life also underwent radical changes. In 1939 his mother and younger brother, who remained in Poland after he and his older siblings had left, were sent by the Soviets in cattle cars to Jambyl, Kazakhstan, where they later died of illness and starvation, likely around 1942. His older sister survived the Nazi blitzes of London with her son, Maurice, and was struggling with mental health aggravated by the trauma of war. And his older brother, who had helped him immigrate to the United States and supported him during his first years, died of a heart attack in early 1944. His ex-lover, Runia Pontsh—who had given birth to Singer's only son, Israel Zamir, in 1929—was expelled from the USSR by the Soviets and, after a sojourn in Istanbul, settled in Palestine in 1938, where a few years later Zamir became a young member of Kibbutz Beit Alfa. In 1940 Singer married a German-Jewish refugee, Alma Wassermann, who had fled with her husband and children from Munich, and who, after meeting him at a Catskills summer resort, began an affair that led to leaving her husband and starting a new life with the unknown Yiddish writer. Singer became a citizen of the United States in 1943, solidifying his commitment to finding a path in literature as an American writer.

This biographical background is helpful in understanding the intensity of Singer's writing during this time. The topics, while covering various aspects of Yiddish culture and Jewish life, are all infused with his personal perspective and experience at the time they were written. This makes his wartime work fundamentally different from almost everything published to date—nearly thirty books for adults and more than fifteen for children in English translation alone. It opens a new phase in the translation and publication of Singer's writing, exposing an immediacy and rawness that were, during his lifetime, mediated by the length of time that passed between the writing and translation of a given piece, as well as editorial and cultural concerns reflecting his contemporary American context. The gap between Singer's Yiddish and English publications, which greatly influenced his decisions, is partly closed, offering readers more direct access to his perspective on life in the old country from which he came and the new country where he settled.

One of the most important aspects of this access is the chronological order in which the pieces have been organized. It is the usual practice for authors to publish their work in the order that it is written, as Singer did in Yiddish. But since Singer translated his work into English after it was written, often publishing it out of order, American readers were less often able to engage with his writing chronologically. His first short story collection, *Gimpel the Fool and Other Stories* (1957), featured stories that were originally published, in order of their appearance in the English version, in 1945, 1957, 1945, 1956, 1956, 1945, 1956, 1943, 1932, 1956, and 1943. Anyone trying to get a sense of Singer's development as a writer from the arc of the stories as they appeared in the collection would go dizzy bouncing back and forth between the early 1940s and the mid-1950s, making a pit stop in the early 1930s, all without an inkling of what he wrote in between. This non-sequentiality lent a sense of mystery to Singer's writing. But it did little to offer readers a coherent view of the author's artistic vision.

This volume takes the opposite approach, following the order in which each article appeared in the *Forverts*. It gives readers a sense of how Singer's thinking on various topics developed over time and grounds each piece in its immediate historical context. Still, the nature of their composition—being written quickly for newspaper readers—means that the kind of editing that Singer undertook with other published works was left undone. With this in mind, the pieces have all been edited for clarity and concision, without altering the writing itself, through careful selection, indicated in the text by ellipses. In addition, short introductory paragraphs provide exact publication dates as well as historical, cultural, or biographical information, offering additional context. In all, the pieces speak for themselves, and their overall coherence issues from Singer's focus when approaching his topics and themes.

The twenty-five pieces included in this volume were selected from a pool of over 150 potential articles. These numbers make it clear that the selection is representative rather than comprehensive—an embarrassment of riches. More could certainly have been included. The decision to limit them was based on a desire to keep the volume itself focused on a coherent yet varied set of topics. While the pieces appear in chronological order, only about a third appeared between 1939 and 1943 and the rest in 1944 and 1945—during the last two years of World War II and its immediate aftermath. This ratio results from an increasing number of pieces written about Yiddish culture and Jewish life as news spread of the destruction of Jewish life in Europe. It also reflects an editorial aim, in collecting this volume, to underscore the impact of the Holocaust on Singer's consciousness.

The articles vary across several themes connected to Jewish life and Yiddish culture, including history, customs, the influence of particular individuals, social tendencies, and critiques of the moment in which Singer was living and writing. The challenges in translating this material are different from those of translating literary fiction. Whereas fiction demands being attuned to the aesthetic qualities of language, nonfiction demands, in addition to aesthetic considerations, the consistency of thought and formulation that is present in any critical text. Nowhere are these challenges more apparent than in the word that appears in the title: yidishkayt.

The Yiddish word *yidishkayt*, which is spelled Yiddishkayt in English, has many meanings and connotations, making it nearly impossible to apply a single solution to each usage. It can mean Judaism, Jewish life, anything having to do with Yiddish culture or language, and, in its most vague sense, can be Jewishness or even Yiddishness. Max Weinreich, the legendary Yiddish linguist and historian who headed the YIVO Institute for Jewish Research, broached this topic in the opening paragraph of his seminal article "*Yidishkayt* and Yiddish" (1953), from which the thematic focus of this volume takes some of its inspiration. Weinreich wrote:

Religion, as used in this paper with reference to Ashkenazic Jewry, is to be understood in its most inclusive sense. Today, there are many aspects of

Jewishness that are not necessarily religious. But in traditional Ashkenazic Jewry, it must be firmly kept in mind, religion was no part time job, no Saturday versus Sunday pastime, as it happens to be in some cases today. It was a way of life and, even more important, an outlook on life. I know of no word that would convey this idea of inclusiveness as cogently as the Yiddish term for Jewishness, *yi'dishkayt*.

Yiddish and *yidishkayt* can be simultaneously both cultural and religious terms. They also betray their inherent "Ashkenocentrism"—the implicit links between Yiddish culture and language and Jewish life in central and eastern Europe as distinct from Jewish life in any other part of the world, especially North Africa and the Middle East. As such, while emphasizing the centrality of Yiddish to the popular notion of American Judaism, the collection makes that cultural context more specific, marking its difference from other forms of Jewish life, culture, and religion.

Yiddishkayt can be an essence, a quality, a general state of being Ashkenazically Jewish, but it can also refer to Judaism as a religion practiced by Ashkenazi Jews. When Singer writes, "Our parents and grandparents studied Yiddishkayt their whole lives," he means *Judaism* rather than any other vague notion of the word. But when he writes, "there cannot be . . . any kind of peace between fascism and Yiddishkayt," he refers specifically to the spirit of Jewish life, which he believes is antithetical to fascist power. And when he writes elsewhere that "many modern Jews feel that Yiddishkayt is a bit of bad luck and nothing else," he refers precisely to being Jewish as something that is, in essence, vague. So throughout this volume, the same Yiddish word, *yidishkayt*, is rendered differently in different instances—and, in some cases, is reproduced simply as "Yiddishkayt."

This ambiguity is actually built into the Yiddish word *yidish*, which can mean either "Jewish" or "Yiddish." Most times, the meaning of the word is clear from the context, but sometimes it is not, and what is often missing in translation is precisely the ambiguity between the two—the fact that when we render the word *Yidish* in English as "Jewish," we can *also* refer, in some ways, to a measure of Yiddish language and culture.

As for the core themes in this volume, those that emerge most tangibly are the anger and anxiety that Singer felt over the apparent indifference of the Jewish sphere—including in the Yiddish world—over the cultural treasures that were in the process of being lost during World War II. Understanding his literary mission in the years during and after the Holocaust involves a reading of those concerns that he articulated during the time that it was actually taking place. It is no surprise, reading these pieces, that his first literary project after the end of the war was to write an epic novel about Jewish life in Poland. The pieces in this collection make it clear that, for Singer, this Jewish life was not an abstract idea. It was a visceral loss not only of the environment in which he grew up but also of the two figures most directly associated with his own personal upbringing: his mother, who spent the most time raising him, and his older brother, who, in many senses, was the closest figure he had to a father.

These circumstances imbue this volume of Singer's wartime writings with an intensely urgent tone. Singer did not have time to waste in writing the articles that he published during this period. He wanted to get it all on record—not only the customs but also the immediacy of the loss that he realized was taking place at that very moment. Knowing that a whole world, a whole way of life, a whole cultural treasure bound up with Yiddish and Yiddishkayt were all going up in flames before his very eyes—this knowledge was crushing for Singer. It also drove him to put pen to paper and write.

—David Stromberg, Jerusalem

This first article represents Singer's return to publishing bylined articles after a two-year hiatus during which he wrote an anonymous popular digest column called "It's Good to Know." Later in his career, he claimed to have suffered a creative block during this period, and indeed he published no fiction between April 1937 and July 1943—a long lapse for a writer who became immensely prolific. But in March 1939 he began publishing book reviews under his known pseudonym, Yitskhok Bashevis, in *Tsukunft*, a monthly literary journal acquired by the *Forverts* in 1912 and edited by Avrom Liessin until his death in 1938, at which point it was edited by Samuel Charney, a friend who possibly gave Singer the chance to return to serious cultural criticism. By April 1939 Singer had also began publishing long articles in the *Forverts* using the pseudonym Yitskhok Varshavski, Isaac from Warsaw. The first few retold the histories of famous Jewish historical figures, including philosopher Salomon Maimon (1753-1800) and Jewish leader Zalman Wolfowitz (1711-1757), also known as the "Dictator of Drohobyzc." By July Singer was supplementing his histories with descriptions of various aspects of Jewish life and culture from the old country, offering contemporary *Forverts* readers a view into the customs of their forebears. The first was about *agunot*, "chained" wives who cannot remarry. This marks Singer's turn from historical to cultural topics, showing his tendency to consider these two facets of the past in relation to each other. The decision to open this collection with this piece reflects Singer's later interest in those aspects of traditional Jewish life that led to complications or difficulties where individual fates were concerned. With war in Europe on the horizon, it also marks Singer's attempts to thematize the problems of the past using the quandaries of the present and imminent future.

Agunot–Wives of Missing Husbands Not Allowed to Remarry by Jewish Law

(July 16, 1939)

For many years now, the *Forverts* has published a "gallery" of different sorts of men, some of which leave their wives and children and go off to some faraway place to flee or disappear. There are different reasons for why these men run off. Sometimes it's because of a spiteful wife who wants to fight all the time. Sometimes it's because a man has fallen in love with another woman. It also happens that a man leaves his wife and children to become a vagrant, a drifter. Every case has its reasons.

According to American law, when a man leaves a woman and doesn't return after a certain amount of time, the woman is granted a divorce through the courts and can marry someone else. "Desertion" is one of the most important grounds for divorce in many states in America and in other countries as well. *Din*, the Jewish law of the Torah, is completely different. According to religious law, a Jewish woman can only be granted a divorce by her husband. If the man has disappeared and no one knows where he has gone, the woman remains an aguna. She can't marry anyone else. She has to live out her years alone.

But a woman becomes an aguna not only when a man disappears. There are cases in which a man dies, or is killed, and the woman still remains an aguna. If a man drowns in the sea, the woman should—according to the law of the Talmud—not remarry, even if witnesses saw the man fall into the water and not come out. The rabbis who wrote this law believed that it was possible for a sea current to carry her husband somewhere far off and then wash him ashore on an island. The fact that a man fell into the water and did not come out was, in such a case, not yet proof that he was dead. This was the belief of the Tannaim, the rabbinic sages of the Talmud. This is why the woman was never allowed to remarry.

Moreover, if a man falls into a river and is pulled out after drowning, the woman can still be an aguna—if fish have eaten off the drowned man's nose. The woman could have a thousand indications that the drowned man is her husband. Yet the Tannaim believed that people can only be identified by their foreheads and noses. If the nose is gone, there's no proof that this is the same person. The fact that a woman recognizes a man's clothes, his hands, feet, neck, shoulders, has no significance. According to religious law, she remains an aguna.

We can think what we want about these laws, but it's a fact that for almost two thousand years, Jews have lived according to them, and many religious Jews still live this way today. In Poland, in Romania, and in other countries where there are religious Jews, there are still agunot today. Thousands of religious Jewish women whose husbands have disappeared or died at war remain alone their whole lives. In the Jewish shtetls of Poland and Lithuania, an aguna is very much a common occurrence. The number of agunot grew especially large after the Great War. The fact that the military had sent a letter saying that a soldier had been killed at the front was not always enough for the rabbis to allow a woman to remarry. Each case had to be looked into separately. Thousands of young Jewish women whose husbands were killed at war remained agunot. They preferred living a life of misery to losing the *Olam Ha'Ba*, the world to come.

But what happens today is nothing compared to what happened once, in the past, when all Jews lived religious lifestyles and the rabbis completely ruled the Jewish street. In those days, there was no Jewish town that didn't have a few or even many agunot. And there was no Yiddish *Forverts* then to help find lost husbands. When a husband argued with his wife, and wanted to say the worst possible thing to her, something that would really make her suffer, he would often say, "I'll go away and leave you a lonely aguna!" Such a threat left a Jewish woman scared to death. When a Jewish man left on a long journey, his wife begged God not only for his health and life but also that she, God forbid, not be left an aguna. The fear of becoming an aguna has always loomed ominously over Jewish women.

When Jews first started immigrating to America, people treated the women left behind in the old country like agunot. Very often, rabbis asked men who were immigrating to divorce their wives. You could never be sure whether the immigrant would bring his wife over to America. You could never be sure that the ship wouldn't sink. You could never really be sure of anything. The husband could have loved his wife and been a loyal husband and father. Still, he had to leave his wife a bill of divorce. Later, when he brought her to America, they remarried . . .

Rabbis were always busy with agunot. Many thousands of religious books were written about agunot. Very often, the aguna was thirteen or fourteen years old. Jews married off their children very young, at twelve or thirteen, and often even younger. In some towns, the custom was for young men to go to yeshiva after getting married. Why should they sit at home? Their eleven- or twelve-year-old wives, who were themselves children, played with other kids. Such a young boy was of no use in business either. Instead of sitting and listening to his mother-in-law's insults, he quickly took some of the dowry and went off to study Torah. But some of these boys got lost on their journeys, and no one knew where they'd ended up. One could have gotten sick somewhere with smallpox along the way and died in a poorhouse. Another went swimming in a river and drowned. It was just as easy to find those who simply ran away.

Many thirteen- and fourteen-year-old agunot are mentioned in *she'elot-ve'tshuvot*, questions and answers exchanged by rabbis. It's hard to convey the experience of such a child! The older she was, the better she understood her own tragedy. Married women shook their heads at her. Unmarried women pointed their fingers. It was no use for her parents to run to the rabbis, crying, begging, or saying that, surely, special permission could be given to their child to remarry. The rabbis wanted to help, and they sympathized with their misfortune, but the letter of the law was against them . . .

As with the first article in this volume, which emphasizes Singer's interest in the problematic meeting points between religious tradition and individual fates, this one foregrounds another facet of Singer's long-standing thematic interests: demonology and its place in Ashkenazi Jewish society throughout its history. The article reveals Singer's unique approach to the demonic in Jewish culture: balancing what may be called its social and psychological elements alongside its interplay with faith and superstition. The article is considerably edited, as large portions of the original involve retelling dybbuk stories, including the famous tales of Rabbi Shmelke of Nikolsburg, who told of an exorcism he witnessed after a yeshiva student living in his town was possessed. The stories of these possessions and exorcisms are widely available, and Singer himself would later adapt and reinvigorate the genre of the dybbuk tale in his own fiction. The article, as presented here, focuses on how Singer conceptualized the dybbuk in Jewish society as well as how these tales reflect questions of mental health in his time. This and the previous piece are the only articles in this collection to appear before the outbreak of World War II.

What Is a Dybbuk?

(July 30 and August 6, 1939)

When we were children, we were sometimes told stories about dybbuks. The stories were more or less similar to each other. They dealt with sinful souls that entered into young men or women. The soul belonged to a sinful person who'd died long ago. Because of these sins, the dead person's soul would wander after death, unable to find rest and looking for any chance to possess a living person. The way these stories usually transpired, the sinful soul always picked a man or a woman who was young. We never heard about sinful souls possessing an old man or an old woman.

Young people who'd become enlightened, read worldly books, and cast religious observance aside usually laughed at stories about dybbuks. They argued that there was no such thing as a soul that existed without a body, and so, as a result, there could be no such thing as a dybbuk. They argued that those whom others took for "dybbuks" were simply and completely crazy or else pretending. This explanation was extremely offensive to the religious sentiment of the older generation, but the younger generation stood their ground. There were also those who said that there was no such phenomenon as a dybbuk and that the stories about them were completely invented, falsified, and faked.

We can obviously give no answer to the question of

whether a soul can live or exist after the body dies and whether, generally speaking, there is such a thing as a soul. These questions belong to the "eternal questions" for which humanity can offer no answers. Moreover, the German philosopher Emmanuel Kant showed in his work that these three questions—Is there a God? Is there a soul that lives after death? And are there rewards for our good deeds and punishments for our sins?—that, as far as these three questions are concerned, philosophy will never be able to determine who is right, the believer or the unbeliever.

We only want to say here that the belief that sinful souls enter other people's bodies after death is a very ancient one and that it did not originate with Jews. In India this belief is thousands of years old. If the inhabitants of India do not eat meat, it's because they believe that every creature has a human soul. Eating an ox, a cow, or a chicken, therefore, means eating a human being. Belief in reincarnation—that is, the possibility that the soul of someone dead can enter that of a living person—also spread quickly among Christians during the Middle Ages. Stories about dybbuks were told not only by our grandmothers and grandfathers but across the whole world, among Christians, among Hindus, among Buddhists, and among Muslims too. During the Middle Ages, dybbuks were more popular among Christians than Jews. There are thousands of documents that describe dybbuks entering young Christian men and women and how religious priests banished them with "holy water," prayers, and invocations. The stories that were told about Christian dybbuks were strangely similar to those told about Jewish dybbuks.

The more you read about these events, and interest yourself in them, the more you come to the conviction that the issue at hand isn't simply a bluff, an invented story that has no root in reality. The descriptions are often very precise. They give names, dates, and many other details. The documents were often also signed by local officials. Among Jews, dybbuks were often described by famous rabbis and scholars. You could say that these rabbis were superstitious or fanatical, but it is impossible to say that they were outright liars. Something had to have taken place. Everyone could not be complete liars.

Doctors and psychologists who are interested in these questions have almost all come to the same conclusion: the dybbuks described by Christians and Jews were cases of a nervous condition called hysteria.

Hysteria is a broad concept. When a woman begins screaming in a high voice, crying, laughing, or making a scene, we usually say that she is being hysterical. But there are cases of hysteria that are much more acute and complicated. Sometimes men or women are suddenly paralyzed and can't move either their hands or their feet. Yet when the doctors begin to look for some ailment, they come to the conclusion that the people are not paralyzed in the usual sense of the word but that they have a hysterical paralysis, the result of nervous shock. In reality, such people can walk and move their hands and feet. There is no bodily organ that's sick. But certain events can have such an effect on people that they don't *want* to talk. They no longer believe in their own power. They're afraid to move their hands and feet. If such people suddenly saw that the house they were in caught on fire, and that they were in danger of burning to death, they would immediately begin to run. They'd forget all about their paralysis. This is why people usually assume that hysterics are pretending—that they're playing a part.

There is a great amount of truth in this assessment. Hysterics are, in reality, actors of sorts—they are like performers. They like to exaggerate their suffering. They want people's attention. They want doctors to come all the time and examine them. No one took care of them. When people like this are paralyzed as a result of hysterics, they aren't satisfied with lying in one place and being cared for. They scream, cry, complain, and want as many people as possible to know that they're sick. Doctors have precise indicators to distinguish between hysterics and people who have a "real" or organic illness. The eyes of those who are truly blind don't react to light. You can shine a flashlight ten times in front of their open eyes. They know nothing about it—it doesn't bother them. It is completely different with those who are hysterically blind. If you were to shine a flashlight or electric bulb in their eyes, their pupils would contract. These people are convinced—and have convinced others—that they are blind. They believe, and they make others believe, that they can't see, and as a result they really do not see for a certain period of time. But their eyes can see and are sensitive to light.

Hysterics often display behaviors that cause normal people, but not doctors, to be afraid. They bang their heads on the wall, grind their teeth, make terrible faces, and reveal a level of strength of which we would not have believed them capable. Hysterics are unconscious liars. They play out a comedy without knowing that they are playing it out. Hysterics often fast for weeks at a time, but close monitoring shows that they sneak food. It's interesting that hysterics are very often cautious and would never do something that would really harm them. Hysterics will bang their heads on the wall but never with enough strength to fracture their skulls. Hysterics will bruise themselves up but will rarely cut open their veins.

Hysterics are usually people within whom too much unused energy has been pent up. A nervous shock has the effect of turning this pent-up energy into a sickness and releasing it as hysteria. People who have jobs, lead normal sex lives, have friends and socialize rarely become hysterical. In olden days, when rich women did not do anything for themselves and had nowhere to direct the great amount of life force that lived in them, there were many hysterics among them. The modern woman who studies, works, is active, travels, and socializes has as little chance of suffering from hysteria as a modern man.

Life in the Middle Ages was a breeding ground for hysterics. Religious fanaticism, all kinds of superstitions, the constant fear of plagues, ghosts, and demons, the immense mortality that ruled this period, the terrible hygienic conditions, the uncertainty of knowing how you'd feed yourself, how to stay healthy—all this together created conditions in which hysteria could very easily develop. Above all, belief in dybbuks suited hysterics perfectly.

Today, when a woman becomes hysterical, she is sent off to a hospital, and this takes care of everything. But in the Middle Ages, hysterics could play out their performances, their comedies, on a grander scale. The hysterics who garnered the most attention were those who played the "dybbuk." When a quiet Jewish maiden suddenly started screaming, throwing herself around, and acting as if a sinful soul were speaking through her, she didn't have to worry about publicity. The word *dybbuk* inspired a ghastly fear in people. The entire town, both Jews and Christians, would quickly come running. Just as good actors grow into their roles at the moment when they sense that there is a great audience before them— that their performance is being admired, that people believe in their talent and in their craft—just in the same way the hysterical woman grows into her role as a "dybbuk." Not only did she make others believe that a sinful soul was speaking through her, but she believed it herself. The lie soon became the truth. She cried out with a voice that wasn't her own. She enumerated sins that no one had ever imagined she could have known about. She beat her breast, confessed, pulled the hair out of her head, and raised such a racket, screeching so loudly, that the entire shtetl shuddered.

In documents about dybbuks, left behind by rabbis and priests, it is said that dybbuks had great strength, which the rabbis and priests describe as supernatural. But doctors know that common hysterics often reveal unbelievable strength. For hysterics, all of this energy, all of this attention, is directed at one point, and this gives them strength that is far above average . . .

It is a common occurrence for hysterics to begin speaking in foreign languages. Many studies have been carried out looking into this phenomenon. All of the doctors and psychologists who have dealt with this question have come to the same conclusion: that the "foreign" languages in which they spoke were not foreign to them at all. Once, many years ago, they had been able to speak these languages, had acquaintances who used these languages, or were brought up in houses where the servants spoke these languages. Many American children hear their parents speak Yiddish, but they themselves never learn to speak Yiddish. But if an American woman, whose parents spoke Yiddish to each other, were to fall into an acute state of hysteria, it would not be out of the question for her suddenly to begin speaking in good and clear Yiddish.

Where do hysterics get such a talent for languages? The answer is that when people find themselves in a hysterical condition, the part of consciousness that begins to act out, the part that comes into action, is the *unconscious*. Long-forgotten events come up to the memory's surface. Those experiences to which we pay little attention under normal circumstances, and which we appear to have forgotten, come back to life. These same experiences resurface in our dreams. People whom we haven't seen for decades, and whom we seem to completely have forgotten, often appear lifelike in our dreams. Modern psychology teaches that, in essence, we forget nothing. Somewhere in the depths of our minds we keep all of our experiences, everything we've seen and heard, everything we've learned and experienced. In our dreams, or in hysterical conditions, that which has for many years laid repressed and hidden comes to the surface . . .

Just as actors are sometimes taken over by their own

performances, caught up in their very own acting and ready to cry the bitterest tears over the tragic fate of the characters they play—in this very same way, and even more so, hysterics are taken up by their "roles." In the end, actors are normal people who always know that they are acting. Hysterics are completely different. They act without knowing that they're acting. They take their role seriously. The young men and women who declared themselves to be possessed by dybbuks believed that real sinful souls had entered into them, and they slowly came to live with these sinful souls, becoming friendly with them, as close as family . . .

Like the first two pieces in this collection, this one also foregrounds one of Singer's core interests: the tradition of Jewish mysticism known as the Kabbalah. Singer was raised in a household imbued with Hasidic Kabbalah, which issued mainly from the kabbalistic teachings of Rabbi Isaac Luria of Safed. According to Singer's later testaments, he read kabbalistic texts from a young age, despite knowing that it was considered taboo for Jews to study the secrets of the Torah before the age of forty. During the 1920s, as a young man living in Warsaw, Singer also joined the circle of intellectuals who spent time with Hillel Zeitlin, a writer and poet who closely followed the field of study being developed at the time by Gershom Scholem—the preeminent modern scholar of Kabbalah. Singer also showed his own understanding of Kabbalah, including its role in Eastern European Jewish cultural history, in 1933, with the serial publication of his first novel, *Satan in Goray*, which focused on the teachings of false messiah Sabbatai Zevi, who exploited kabbalistic teachings for his own gains. This article, which acts as a primer for *Forverts* readers, combines Singer's personal conception of Kabbalah with the more academic approach that had been developed throughout the 1930s. A year into the onslaught of World War II, Singer appears to be moving beyond considerations of cultural or social phenomena to the notions that guided Jewish spiritual life throughout times of great crisis.

What Is Kabbalah?

(October 6, 1940)

For many hundreds of years, the word *Kabbalah* has evoked a holy trembling among Jews across the whole world. A *mekubal*, a kabbalist, was someone who people believed knew the secrets of the world's creation, and though he roamed through the sinful earth just like everyone else, he also knew what was happening in the heavens.

Wondrous tales of people who knew mysterious teachings were already told in the Talmud. The Gemara of the Megillah Tractate tells the story of a man who could create a calf using the Holy Names. The Gemara of the Hagigah Tractate says that average people should not delve into the mysteries of the world and that those who tried to look into the secrets of divinity came to harm because of such attempts. The belief that the Torah consists not only of simple stories and commandments but also of deep secrets is very old. It's believed that Jews received much of their mysterious knowledge in Egypt, Babylon, and Persia. There are elements in the Kabbalah that prove they originate from ancient times.

The word *Kabbalah*, in the sense of mysterious knowledge, first appeared in Hebrew literature in the eleventh century. Kabbalah means *receiving*. The kabbalists believe that the secrets of the Torah were already received by Jews at Mount Sinai. At the time when the

Torah was put into writing so that it could be studied by everyone, the Kabbalah was given only to those few people who, through their piety, merited having the secrets of the Torah revealed to them. These select few gave the secrets over to other select few. Still, some of these people did put these secrets into writing. There's a kabbalistic book that the kabbalists say was written by Abraham. It's called *Sefer Yetsira*, the Book of Creation. Another book is said to have been written by Enoch—the same Enoch who religious Jews believe ascended to the heavens alive. The Hebrew Bible says that God took him away. This same Enoch plays an important role in the Kabbalah. The Christian mystics, as well as the Gnostics, considered him important as well.

The Kabbalah is not a unified form of knowledge. It developed over many hundreds of years. All the great kabbalists had their own systems, their own conceptions. It goes without saying that no kabbalist has ever been to heaven. The Kabbalah is a product of the human imagination, the human desire to penetrate mystery and to reveal what is hidden. While philosophers made use of their intelligence to study life and the world, the kabbalists made use of their imaginations. The kabbalists had deeply religious natures. They believed that when people live pure lives, when they fast, when they don't give in to their passions and instead pray to God, there's a chance for them to discover things that simple people will never know. There were kabbalists who fasted by day for many years and only ate small meals at night. Others fasted from one Shabbat to the next. Many kabbalists went outdoors naked on winter nights and rolled around in snow, and in this way tried to purify themselves from sin. There were also kabbalists who forsook living in cities and lived in huts out in the fields. They believed that the pure air and proximity to nature helped them apprehend the hidden and the divine.

For hundreds of years, there have been two different types of Kabbalah. The first type consisted of *theoretical* Kabbalah, the Kabbalah that set for itself no other purpose but a search for the pure truth. The second category consisted of *practical* Kabbalah. Many kabbalists wanted to use their Kabbalah to achieve practical ends. They believed that through the power of Kabbalah, they could create calves and doves—that through Kabbalah they could draw wine from walls and take seven-mile steps. They also believed that, through Kabbalah, they could heal all kinds of illnesses and even resurrect the dead. The practical kabbalists were, in a certain sense, similar to alchemists—people who tried to turn lead into gold.

It's interesting that, despite the fact that there were different kabbalists in different times and that they each had their own systems, a kabbalistic worldview nevertheless developed over time, a kind of kabbalistic philosophy.

According to the Jewish religion, God created the world from nothing. God simply said that there should be a world, and a world came into being. The Torah begins with the words that God created the heavens and the earth. But many ancient philosophers who actually believed in God thought that even God didn't have the power to create a world out of nothing. There had to be some primordial matter from which God created the world. One possibility was that the Godhead created the world from itself. The Godhead removed a part of its divine substance and this substance slowly transformed into earth, water, and everything that we have in the world. The kabbalists adopted this belief. The world that we see is, according to the kabbalists, not simply the kind of world that was created by some sort of divine whim but is itself a part of the Godhead.

The Kabbalah teaches that before God created the world, everything was filled with divinity. The Godhead was alone. It had existed since time immemorial. Naturally, we can't apprehend just what kind of substance divinity is made from, but the kabbalists believed that it is a spiritual substance. The kabbalists speak very little about divinity itself. The only thing they can say about it is that we know nothing.

In order for the world to be created, God had to make room for a world. Divinity had to shrink. A kind of emptiness had to be created. So the first act of the world's creation was the Godhead's limiting of itself, its own shrinking. Once there was this empty space, the Godhead removed a part of its own substance, which slowly developed into the world.

In the religious book *Etz Hayim—The Tree of Life*—the legendary kabbalist Rabbi Hayim Vital asks the following question: Why did God create the world? Why did the Godhead have to limit its divinity to create a world? The answer is that as long as the Godhead had not created the world, it lacked certain attributes. The Godhead could only come to be called the Creator once it created the world. Before that it could not have had this name. If the Godhead was to be called king, it had to reign over someone. There can be no king without a world. So the world's creation was necessary for divinity to grow—for it to include all possible attributes.

And yet the world will not last forever. A day will come when everything that exists will slowly return to divinity. A day will come when divinity will again fill everything. Total divinity is total understanding, total bliss, total rest. Kabbalah is an optimistic teaching. It says that no matter how much trouble and suffering we go through in the world, the end will be good. We come from divinity, and to divinity we will return.

The kabbalists placed a lot of emphasis on the other side of divinity—on the world of Satan and the evil spirits. For the world to be able to exist in its current form, the principle of evil had to be created. Just as there cannot be light without shadow, so there cannot be a world without evil. According to the kabbalists, evil is present not only in human beings but also in the highest spiritual realms. Evil cannot vanish until the world returns to divinity.

The kabbalists also placed a lot of emphasis on sex. According to the kabbalists, the masculine and feminine principles exist not only among living creatures but also in the highest realms. Two beings must come together for a third being to emerge. Two thoughts have to meet for a third to be born. According to the kabbaliasts, the Godhead has a wife. They call her the *Shekhinah*. This didn't mean that God was married to a woman in the human sense. It means that God too creates according to the principle of coming together, of copulation. Kabbalists believed that since the destruction of the Second Temple, the Shekhinah has been in exile. God can no longer come together with the Shekhinah, and that is why the world is so sad, so uncreative, so dark.

Many kabbalists would wake up in the middle of the night and perform midnight prayers. They'd smear ash on their foreheads and cry and plead with God to make up with the Shekhinah. Then the Messiah would come.

This article represents a new front in Singer's cultural criticism: World War II and its effect on Jewish life and human civilization. As such, it begins Singer's personal war coverage, which conveys not news but the cultural significance of events taking place in Europe. The first article of this kind, "The Hitlerists Now Speak Openly: They Simply Want to Introduce Slavery," appeared on January 5, 1941, and among other articles from this time are "Jews in the Deserts of Africa Where England Is Having One Victory after Another" (February 2), "Our Greatest Danger Is a Hitler Regime in South America" (May 4), and "America and England Have a Plan to Beat the Nazis and Bring About Hitler's Downfall" (August 24). Each of these is interesting in its own right, and a thorough consideration of Singer's war-themed writing would offer insight into how it influenced his work, as well as give a picture of one person's attempts to respond to the cataclysm of World War II as it unfolded. This piece was chosen for what it says about the dangers of underestimating the evil of powerful rulers as well as for how it foregrounds Hitler's view of Jews—and the core values Singer sees in Jewish culture, which, he contends, make it antithetical to fascism.

Jews Would Oppose Nazis Even if Fascists and Hitlerites Were Not Antisemites

(September 7, 1941)

"I had been investigating the activities of the Jewish people," writes Hitler in *Mein Kampf*, "over long periods of human history, when suddenly I became anxious and asked myself: Had destiny not decreed at some point that this small nation should have the final victory?"

In a conversation with Gregor Strasser, Hitler's former friend and follower, Hitler explained that the greatest and mightiest enemy of Nazism was the Jewish people. Hitler said he was more afraid of Jews and Jewish ideas than English warships or the French army. Hitler explained, in a variety of ways, that he was waging war against Jewry and only with Jewry.

There was a time when Hitler's antisemitism wasn't taken very seriously, just as his political program, threats against ethnic groups, and power over the German people were not taken seriously. Hitler was not the first antisemite and will not be the last. As long as Hitler did not put words into action, there was no reason for anyone to take what he said seriously. Many Jewish journalists found all kinds of ways to say that Hitler's antisemitism was nothing more than a demagogical means with which to trap Germany's ignorant masses in his net. Even many German Jews believed that as soon as Hitler came to power, he would put an end to his anti-Jewish propaganda, which would become useless to him. Many politicians expressed the opinion that Hitler had made a mistake in singling out the Jews. Had Hitler not spoken out against the Jews, these politicians said, he would have had many Jewish followers.

But time has shown that Hitler took his program and his views more seriously than anyone could have imagined.

Many non-Jews and even Jews think that his hate is built more on political trickery than on any deep internal sentiment. Many thinking people believe that, were it to serve his interests, Hitler would wake up one fine day and make peace with Jews. What wouldn't a dirty demagogue do if it served his interests? Hadn't the same Hitler first praised the Poles and then called them inferior? Hadn't Hitler signed an agreement with the Bolsheviks when it served him?

It's not inconceivable that Hitler would in reality make temporary peace with the Jews if it were necessary for his plan. But this in no way proves that the battle between Hitler and the Jewish people is incidental. The deeper you look into the events taking place, the more you are inclined to believe that there cannot be, and never will be, any kind of peace between fascism and Yiddishkayt . . .

When Adolf Hitler says that democracy and socialism are *Jewish ideas*, he makes no mistake. Hitler feels with his instinct (and he has very sharp instincts) that, no matter what happens, Jews will never acknowledge the arrogance of dictators and "rule from above." When Hitler says that the existence of Jews is a personal insult to him, he's not pulling it out of thin air. Jews are the living denial of human deities, petty meaningless creatures who want to make themselves into *gods* . . .

Hitler's greatest accusations against the Jews are as follows:

First, Jews do not believe in authority and in rulers. Jews have spread the "poison" of democracy and socialism across the nations.

Second, Jews are internationalists. Jews are constantly interested in what's happening in other countries. For Jews, the entire world is one single nation.

Third, Jews establish a "foreign body" in every country, a state within a state. In every country, Jews have their own institutions, their own customs, their own way of life. They aren't part of the mainstream.

Hitler possesses an extreme hatred against Jewish writers and journalists. Anyone who hasn't been attacked by the Jewish press, says Hitler, has apparently accomplished very little. It's interesting that while saying that you can tell as many lies as you want for patriotic purposes, Hitler also accuses Jewish journalists of lying.

Hitler speaks with a different sort of hatred about so-called Jewish cowardice. Had Jews been alone in the world, says Hitler, they would have disagreements amongst themselves, but never would they end up in a real war, because none of them would sacrifice their lives in battle.

Adolf Hitler, Benito Mussolini, Philippe Pétain, Ion Antonescu, and the fascists in Hungary all set Jewish ideas in opposition to "ideas" of their own.

Jews do not acknowledge authority, but for fascists,

authority is everything. The ruler is everything—the subject is nothing. People are born so that their rulers can do whatever they want with them.

Jewish internationalism is set up in opposition to fascist, narrow-minded nationalism. Yet it's interesting that fascists want to establish an internationalism of their own. Hitler's goal is for each nation to have a ruler but for Germany's ruler to be the ruler of all the other rulers.

In opposition to Jewish individualism, to Jewish freedom, Hitler puts forth a life that is completely controlled from above. The ruler's word, his whim, his desire, must be law for the entire nation.

In opposition to "Jewish cowardice," Hitler puts forth Aryan heroism. The words "You were born to die for Germany" are written above the entrance to several Nazi military camps. "I will lead us to a point," Hitler said to his friend Gregor Strasser, "when Germans will completely stop fearing death. Only when people go willingly to slaughter will fascism have a truly lasting existence."

Hitler's "ideas" did not fall out of the sky. They are built on an ancient cult of heroes and heroism. Hitler wants to bring the veneration of heroes—which is the foundation of idolatry—back to Europe and to the entire world. The strongest is god: this is the substance of the "new ideas" that the fascists have introduced. The war that Hitler is waging against Jews is, at its core, the ancient battle that idolaters have at various times waged against Jews and against the Jewish spirit. The strongest person is god, and might is right—these are the two core principles of both idolatry and fascism.

We can't say that these principles have no appeal for anyone. The average person has respect for power and for the powerful. Even many highly intelligent people show, from time to time, that they have respect for power and the powerful. But the fascists are bad psychologists if they think that you can wash away and erase thousands of years of culture and bring humanity back to the primal and naked forms of idolatry and hero worship.

Just as nudists will never succeed in convincing the human race that we should all walk around naked, so the fascists will never succeed in convincing people that they should, once and for all, strip off all the forms that culture has introduced over thousands of years. Jewish ideas, faith in justice and in morality, and contempt for violence and cruelty have all entered the blood of the human race. People in modern times fear the sword more than anything else. But rarely do they submit to kissing the sword that cuts their throats. The cult of the hero can no longer exist in its ancient form. The "Jewish poison," the Jewish contempt for violence, has had more influence on the world than the fascists can imagine.

Hitler's war is lost—not just in strategic terms but also in terms of its ideas. Hitler, Mussolini, Antonescu, Pétain—they are all, at their core, like the comic "hero" Don Quixote, who tried to become a knight at a time when knights were no longer in style. Fascists have succeeded in temporarily gaining power, but this power must and will soon slip out of their hands . . .

In addition to treating a topic that Singer developed in many of his stories—the question of how ill-matched couples lived together—this article also embodies a criterion for the future of Yiddish literature that he expressed in one of his better-known essays from this period, "Problems of Yiddish Prose in America" (1943). In that essay, Singer argued that "Yiddish writers will increasingly be forced—willingly or unwillingly—to draw material from *sforim*," religious books usually written in Hebrew. This article shows that, in arguing that religious books were full of cultural treasures that could be mined for stories that would interest contemporary readers, Singer was not merely talking about a future method that needed to be applied in Yiddish literature. He was reflecting on an approach he had already deployed in his cultural criticism in the *Forverts*. This return to religious sources appears to have marked his return to writing literary fiction, too, as he told Irving Buchen that the stories he published in 1943 were composed in the year before—the same year this article was written.

Matchmaking, Weddings, and Divorces—
Tragedy and Comedy in Old Jewish Life
(July 26, 1942)

In the *Tsemakh Tsedek*, a religious book published in Vilnius in 1870—that is, seventy-two years ago—the following question is raised:

A Jewish man with a wife and children allowed himself to be persuaded by the Evil Spirit to take a lover. The book does not say where the man lived. He probably lived in Vilnius or in another large city in Lithuania. Since the man had means, he arranged for his lover to have her own house and often came to visit her. The book also doesn't mention whether the wife knew that her husband, the father of her children, had a lover. The man had maintained his lover this way for over twenty years, and she had borne him a daughter. This daughter was obviously considered illegitimate. After twenty years of living together, the love between the two came to an end. Perhaps the man had grown too old, or perhaps he lost his wealth and could no longer maintain his lover. Meanwhile, his lover met another man who was ready to marry her. The question was whether the man needed to give the woman a *get*, a religious bill of divorce, before she could get married, or whether she could marry without a *get*.

This question was printed in a religious book published seventy-two years ago. Do we need any more proof that people of all times have had the same weak points and that the Evil Spirit does not only torment us today but also had power over our grandparents and great-grandparents?

The *Tsemakh Tsedek* answers that it would be better for the man to give his lover a *get*. It adds that to preserve the respect of the man, his lover, and his wife, the divorce should be arranged quietly. If possible, the man should not put the *get* in the woman's hand but should rather send a messenger.

And here is another question:

A housewife had a maidservant who was thirteen years old. Once, the housewife sent her off to buy five grochens' worth of yeast for baking hallah and gave her a ten-groschen bill, telling her to bring back five groschens in change. After getting the yeast, the maidservant gave the shopkeeper's wife her ten-groschen bill and got a five-groschen bill in return. But the bill was tattered, and since the maidservant wasn't one to let others take advantage of her, she returned both the yeast and the tattered bill. The shopkeeper's wife threw the ten-groschen bill back at her, and it seemed that there would be no sale.

Suddenly the shopkeeper called out, "I have a good bill. Come back." The maidservant returned, presented the ten-groschen bill to his wife, and she gave her back the yeast. When the girl then stretched out her hand for the shopkeeper to give her the "good" bill, he said to her, "*Harei at mekudeshet li b'finfer ze k'dat Moshe v'yisrael*"— meaning that, with this five-groschen bill, you are now my wife according to Jewish religious law. In other words, the man had married her. Had the maidservant immediately, right on the spot, thrown away the bill and said that she did not want to be his wife, everything would have been fine and proper, since a man cannot marry a woman against her will. But the maidservant said nothing. She had probably not understood the whole trick in the first place. The shopkeeper's wife began to cry out. There was a commotion among the other customers in the shop. They knew the law, which said that when a man gave a woman a ring or money, and then said "*Harei at*," she became his wife. The fact that the shopkeeper already had a wife meant nothing according to religious law, since the law allowed a man to marry two wives. One of the customers later bore witness, saying that when the shopkeeper was asked why he did such a thing, he answered, *Well, so I'll have two wives.*

The maidservant did not end up going home with the yeast. She was taken straight to the rabbi. The shopkeeper was brought to the rabbi too. The shopkeeper said that he had only meant it as a joke. The maidservant cried bitter tears and claimed she knew nothing. The man had given her a five-groschen bill, and so she took it. The issue facing the rabbi was whether or not the man needed to give the maidservant a *get*. As long as there was no answer to this question, she was not allowed to marry anyone else. She was considered a married woman.

Such religious questions were often encountered among Jews. A young man gave a young woman a few groschens, a ring, a wristwatch, or whatever, and then said "*Harei at*," and, just like that, this led to all kinds of troubles. The young woman would be dragged to the rabbi, questioned, and very often forced to accept a *get*. Though she had never been with a man, she was considered a divorced woman. This was obviously not considered an advantage when it came to matchmaking. She was not allowed to marry a Cohen, someone descended from the priestly cast, since a Cohen could not marry a divorced woman.

But the maidservant in this story was lucky. Her luck consisted in the fact that the five-groschen bill that the man had given her was actually hers, not his. He had given it to her as change for a ten-groschen bill that she had given him, and since according to law the ring or the money with which a man consecrated a woman had to belong to *him*, the "*Harei at,*" in this case, had no consequence. And so, according to religious law, the young woman remained unmarried. She managed to get off with only fear, shame, and dishonor . . .

And here's a story about a young girl who was forced to marry against her father's will and the tragedy to which it led. In a shtetl in Lithuania lived a man named Reb Shimshen who was still relatively young. His eldest daughter was about eleven years old. One day a certain young man arrived in town, a divorcé or a widower, and the little girl caught his eye. Soon he sent a matchmaker to Reb Shimshen telling him he wanted to marry his daughter. Reb Shimshen wouldn't hear of such a thing. He felt that an eleven-year-old girl could stay with her parents a while longer. There was no rush to marry her off. Also, he didn't like the young man, and, anyway, he felt that were was no reason for him to marry his eleven-year-old daughter off to a young man who was twice her age or even older. In short, Reb Shimshen said no. But Reb Shimshen had a wife, and she immediately grew attached to the idea of a match. As much as Reb Shimshen made every effort to show her that it was neither a good nor a practical match, so his wife did everything possible to show him that it was simply the best possible match, and that if they didn't marry the eleven-year-old girl off now, she could end up an old maid. This led to such heated discussions, such arguments and accusations, that Reb Shimshen finally told his wife, "You want to marry her off, so marry her off, but I will not come to such a wedding. I won't hear of such a son-in-law." Reb Shimshen's wife decided that her husband, the stubborn mule, would come to terms with it. He wouldn't go and spoil his daughter's wedding. In short, the engagement contract was drawn up, and soon afterward the wedding was celebrated. The father kept his word. He was not at the wedding. On the day of the wedding he disappeared somewhere, and no one knows where he went.

Soon after the wedding the father returned. The newlyweds were set up in a separate room, but the father would not allow the young man to sleep in the same room with his daughter. He yelled at his son-in-law, saying that he should find his own way and that he would not work to feed him. The father and son-in-law fought and argued this way for three weeks. Then, one day, the son-in-law packed his bags and left. He left the eleven-year-old wife an aguna.

People looked for the young man for days, weeks, months, but the young man was nowhere to be found.

Ten years passed. The eleven-year-old bride was now twenty-one. By now it was time for her to have a husband, but she was a sad aguna. And now the father was interested in his daughter having a husband. So he went to the rabbi and asked him to annul the marriage.

Why should the rabbi annul a marriage? Reb Shimshen had a good reason. According to Jewish law, a young girl cannot be married without her father's consent. Since Reb Shimshen never consented, and wasn't even present under the wedding canopy, it meant that the ceremony was not valid. Reb Shimshen also affirmed that man and wife were never alone and that his daughter was as innocent as she was before the wedding. The father's intentions were all very good, and the rabbi could have in theory annulled the marriage. But there was testimony saying that the father had indeed consented. The father allegedly said: "Do what you want. Go to the cantor, if you want, and write up a marriage contract. It has nothing to do with me." These words now played a major role in the young woman's fate. They could be interpreted in such a way as to say that the father had consented to the marriage. He simply didn't want to be present. The town's rabbi could not be sure, so he sent the question to the rabbi who'd written the *Tsemakh Tsedek*, who answered strictly and said that the marriage could not be annulled.

The unhappy wife remained an aguna for the rest of her life, and the blame lay with her mother, who wanted to provide for her daughter as quickly as possible without taking her husband—her daughter's father—into account.

Who knows? Maybe the mother liked the son-in-law so much that she was ready to face every fight and argument to have him in the house? And maybe that's why her husband was so against him? . . .

This is one of many articles that Singer wrote describing the Jewish holiday cycle and the customs associated with each day, including Rosh Hashanah, Yom Kippur, Sukkot, Simhat Torah, Passover, Shavuot, and Tisha B'Av. These articles are all interesting and, like his wartime writings generally, can be read as a single body of work for further study and consideration. They also reflect Singer's sense of urgency in setting down the customs of the past just as the people whose lives were animated by these customs were being massacred on a mass scale. This article was chosen for its focus on the spiritual significance of the month of Elul before the High Holidays and how it sets the stage for what Singer calls a great folk drama—itself set against one of the worst tragedies in Jewish history.

Elul—the Month When "Even a Fish in Water Trembles"

(September 6, 1942)

Every Jewish month has its sign, its symbol. The sign for one month is a lion, another an ox, a third a bow and arrow. The sign of the month of Elul is a virgin. But there was nothing virginal about this Jewish month. The month of Elul was a month of fear, of repentance, of turning the world on its head. Religious Jews believed, and still believe today, that during Rosh Hashanah the divine books are opened in the heavens, and that inscribed in them are those who will live and who will die, who will perish by fire and who by water, who will be rich and who will be poor. During the month of Elul, which comes before Rosh Hashanah, every Jewish person has a chance to repent and in this way attain a good year, a good inscription, out of the heavens. The word "Elul" is mentioned in the Hebrew Bible, in the Book of Nehemiah. In ancient Syria, the month had a musically romantic name, *Ululu*.

Before the month of Elul even started, Jews could sense its arrival. About a week before Elul, learning began in the study house during the evening, by candlelight or oil lamp. This was the first indication that the lightness of summertime was at its end and that more serious times were beginning. On the Shabbat ahead of the month of Elul, the synagogues and study houses were especially packed. Women who did not usually go to Shabbat prayers came to the women's section of the synagogue, and during the monthly prayers the women cried out and really let themselves be heard. Old women went straight into town looking for sins. Jews believed that when sins were committed in a shtetl, this could harm not only the sinner but others as well, since all Jews were responsible for each other. Many sins had to be overlooked during the year. But during Elul, when a fish in water trembled and when everyone's life was at stake, no one could afford the luxury of having sinners in their town.

Old women who sat outside on benches and knit socks became highly efficient at discovering sins. Every Jewish woman had another story to tell. One had seen a maidservant and a teacher's assistant standing by the well and talking to each other. This was suspicious. Who knew, maybe the servant was having an affair with the assistant? Maybe they were kissing in secret? "You have to be careful about what could come of such things!" said the women.

Every shtetl had a river or a stream in which people swam during the summer. Men and women swam separately. It was customary for men and women to swim with their shirts on. The place where women swam was usually far from the place where men swam, and you couldn't see from one to the other. But one old woman told this terrible story: when she went swimming, she noticed that on a little hill, behind the bushes, a few young men were hiding and watching the women swim. The old women looking for sins were often outraged by such events. "It's no wonder," complained the old women while wringing their hands, "that poor little children are dying of smallpox and measles and diphtheria and all kinds of other diseases." And while it was the young men who were peeping, the women nevertheless blamed each other. "Women have to be careful to make sure no one is watching when they get undressed!" argued the old women. "We have to send a guard to keep watch!" Others insisted that a complete end should be put to women's swimming, once and for all, since it can't lead to anything good.

The shofar was blown in the synagogue every day throughout the month of Elul. According to custom, blowing the ram's horn helped to frighten the Evil Spirit. Why in the world would the Evil Spirit be afraid of the sound of the shofar? The answer is that when the Messiah comes, a giant shofar will be blown, and God will vanquish the Evil Spirit. When the Evil Spirit hears the shofar blowing, it thinks that the Messiah has come and that its end is near, and naturally it grows afraid and distraught. But Jews also believed that during Elul, precisely because they were waging war with it, the Evil Spirit was more brazen than ever. The Evil Spirit wants to show that it fears nothing, not the shofar and not the penitential prayers that Jews recite, and it works that much harder to make Jews sin. The Evil Spirit also had its own people in each shtetl, its "fifth columniks," who helped it secretly.

The wagon drivers who would carry passengers from one shtetl to another helped the Evil Spirit considerably, whether willingly or unwillingly. They would pack their wagons full of men and women. The roads were full of mountains and ditches, and every time that the wagon started to toss and shake, the men and women bumped up against each other. The wagon often traveled all night across dark roads or straight through forests. The women talked, laughed. The provincial clowns told all kinds of funny tales, and the Good Spirit, the Angel of Piety, was none the better.

Suspicious things took place, too, in the streets where the poor lived. Paying no attention to the fact that religious men and women were supposed to remain separate, in the poor streets everyone mingled together. Shoemakers' apprentices, tailors' apprentices, hog-bristle brushmakers, and other tradesmen made friends with seamstresses, servants, and even housemaids. You would often see young men and women getting together to dance. In the poor streets you had old maids, women whose husbands had left them, or widows who couldn't remarry, and no matter how cautious or careful you were you couldn't always be on guard. During the month of Elul, the fear that the entire town would end up paying dearly because of hidden sins hung like a sword over the shtetl.

There was only one piece of advice against all of these things—do so many good deeds that they would outweigh the wrongs—and so people did everything they could. Many religious people woke up at dawn to recite psalms and penitential prayers. Women went to cemeteries, pleading with the dead to speak well of them in the next world. Usually, when going to the cemetery, you only pled at the graves of those who were close to you, with your relatives. But during Elul, women would cry over the graves of strangers, too, especially the graves of religious men and women who could do them favors in the next world. Some women would measure the graves using candle wicks. They would later pour wax onto these wicks and make candles for the study house. Old men and women would fast on Mondays and Thursdays throughout the month of Elul. In the poorhouse, Elul was a plentiful season. The sick and poor living in the poorhouse were often forgotten throughout the rest of the year. But during the month of Elul, people had to remember them if they wanted to ensure a year of livelihood. Women sent soups and meats. Religious people came to check whether the sick were lying comfortably and whether their straw mats needed changing. During Elul, more than at any other time of the year, people were afraid of being cursed, afraid of any mean word that escaped an angry mouth . . .

In the past, just as today, there were people with a bad conscience, or as modern psychologists call it, a guilt complex. Some people, just as they do today, felt extremely guilty for sins they'd committed in secret. No one else knew about them, but in their daily life, they suffered from these sins, which they could not forget . . . Penitents would beat their breasts with their fists. Others would rend their clothes as an expression of remorse, as we do when someone dies. They would tear their lapels to show that they were grieving for their sins. Others would lie across the threshold of the study house and ask anyone going in or out to step and spit on them. It sometimes happened that the penitent was the kind of person one would have least expected to commit such a sin.

The woman was often a quiet housewife upon whom no one had cast even the slightest doubt until that moment. Often the husband of the sinning wife was in the study house, and if he was blindly in love and still had faith in his wife he'd jump at the penitential man with clenched fists and cry out that he was lying and making false accusations about a good Jewish woman. It should be noted that it did sometimes happen that the penitent would be lying. Among the penitents there were hysterics with weak nerves and wild imaginations, and they'd invent sins about both themselves and other people. Religious books often brought up cases in which people would confess to sins, but the other side would deny them categorically, swearing they knew nothing about it. Sometimes a supposed penitent had the spiteful intention of using his confession to separate husband from wife. Sometimes they tried to convince people of things that were completely preposterous, or else they exaggerated the events. Such people were taken straight to the rabbi, and they would also bring the women they claimed to have sinned with. The rabbi would inquire into the matter and ask for details. More than once, though a man had confessed in the synagogue to sinning with a woman, the rabbi pronounced that the penitent was a liar, and the woman was able to stay with her husband.

Elul was a dramatic month for Jews—a time of fear and penitence. A time when they accounted for their actions and embarked upon soul-searching. Penitence was undertaken not only by adults but also by children. A young boy would remember that he had once missed the midday prayer and go to his father to confess his sin. Young women who didn't pray throughout the year would start to pray during Elul and come to synagogue.

Many memories from the old country are bound up with the month of Elul and the Days of Awe—the God-fearing days that follow it and lead to a joyful holiday, Simhat Torah. This last holiday was the happy ending of a great folk drama that started with the first day of Elul, arrived at its climax on Yom Kippur, and then brightened up to come to a joyful end.

This article marks a new stage in Singer's writing. Before this, he tended to convey cultural knowledge of the past in a way that was still, to some degree, separate from his writing about the effects of World War II. Here these two topics come together. The article confronts the secular viewpoint of the war held by most *Forverts* readers with the religious viewpoint that Singer knew from his childhood and teenage years. The opening sentence suggests that Singer has been spending time with religious Jews in New York, most likely from the Chabad movement, which had relocated to the United States in 1940 and which Singer references in the piece. The piece shows Singer's ability to consider current events in both pragmatic-historical and mystical-philosophical terms at once—slowly developing a world-view incorporating cultural knowledge with spiritual insights.

Religious Jews Say That the Current War Is the War of Gog and Magog

(June 20, 1943)

These days, we often hear religious Jews say, "The current war is the War of Gog and Magog." We heard similar words in the last world war and . . . in every war. What this means for Jews is that this war is the last. Its end will see the coming of the Messiah.

Who are Gog and Magog? And, anyway, why should there be a War of Gog and Magog before the Messiah comes?

The name Magog is mentioned in the Torah. Noah, as we know, had three sons: Shen, Ham, and Japhet. Magog was Japhet's son.

The race that came from Japhet is today called Aryan. In the Hebrew Bible it says that Japhet's children included Gomer, Magog, Madai, and Javan. One of Gomer's sons was named Ashkenaz. Javen is the Hebrew word for Greece, *yavan*. Madai is a race that got mixed with the Persians, and Ashkenazim are, as Jews believe, Germans. In short, from Japhet came the Greeks, the Persians, and the Germans—or Aryans. Magog was, therefore, an Aryan race too. Obviously, none of this is to be taken scientifically.

The war that Gog and Magog will unleash on Jews is mentioned in a verse of Ezekiel. It's hard to understand from the verse exactly who is Gog and who is Magog.

Certain parts seem to suggest that Magog is a country and that Gog is its ruler, a little like Hitler is the ruler of Germany. But some people suppose that Gog and Magog are two hostile powers that will unite to destroy the Jews, a little like Hitler is now united with Mussolini. This is how the legend leaves it: Gog and Magog will together unleash the last war against the Jews, and both will be defeated . . .

Gog and Magog are mentioned in the Quran, the Muslim holy book, where they're named Yajuj and Majuj. Muslims believe that Yajuj and Majuj are two barbarian races that have long wanted to destroy the world, but that Alexander the Great, the famous Greek emperor, encircled both of these races with a fortified wall. This wall keeps them locked up . . . Arab legend says that before the Day of Judgment comes, the wall will break, and Yajuj and Majuj, or Gog and Magog, will appear near the Sea of Galilee in Palestine. From there they'll make their way to Jerusalem. They will be so barbaric that they'll eat the dead and do other crazy things. This will last as long as it takes them to get to Jerusalem. In Jerusalem, they will be defeated . . .

The connection between the legend of Gog and Magog and the coming of the Messiah is very old. Rabbi Eliezer, the Tanna sage, speaks of the War of Gog and Magog in the context of what is called "the birth pangs of the Messiah's arrival." Rabbi Akiva, another Tanna, says that the War of Gog and Magog will last twelve months. Others say that the war will last seven years . . .

In different times, Jews have called different nations Gog and Magog. When a nation became hostile to Jews and there was soon a war, Jews said that the nation was Gog or Magog. In the Napoleonic era, religious Jews had plenty of evidence that it was the War of Gog and Magog. The fact that Napoleon went to the Land of Israel strengthened this belief. It seemed to many Jews that Gog and Magog would not only fight against the Jews but that they would also fight amongst themselves. So they believed that Napoleon was Gog and that the Russians were Magog, and that this war would end with the redemption of the Jews . . .

No war has fit the prophecy and legend of Gog and Magog as well as the current war. The way the Bible describes Gog's attacks on peaceful nations, ripping them to pieces, goes very well with Hitler's invasion of Poland, France, Belgium, Holland, and Norway. The prophecy that God will rain hailstone, fire, and brimstone matches well with the huge bombs, the so-called blockbusters, that are now being dropped on Nazi heads in Düsseldorf, Dortmund, Essen, Kiel . . . Hitler had a powerful resemblance to Gog when his field marshal, Erwin Rommel, and his army took Tobruk and stood almost at the gates of the Land of Israel. True, Hitler did not enter the Land of Israel, but his setbacks in Africa began near the Land of Israel and were the result of "hailstone, fire, and brimstone"—or the bombs that the English and American airplanes dropped from what might as well have been the heavens.

So we shouldn't be surprised that, despite all of the disappointments that religious Jews have had with earlier wars, the belief is spreading among them that we finally have the true War of Gog and Magog. Many religious people say that Hitler has all the indications of Gog and that Mussolini is the spitting image of Magog.

The Lubavitcher Rebbe, Rabbi Yosef Yitzchak Schneersohn, is sure that Hitler is Gog. It's said that among Lubavitcher Hasidim, a "reception committee" is being established—a group of religious Jews who are preparing to welcome the Messiah after Gog-Hitler dies a violent death. It's hard to say where it's written that the Messiah will appear through a reception committee. But Lubavitcher Hasidim obviously know better.

The kabbalists in the Land of Israel also have a strong belief that this current war is the War of Gog and Magog. There are old Jews, great scholars of Kabbalah, in Jerusalem, in Safed, and in other Jewish cities in the Land of Israel, and they affirm that there can no longer be any doubt. It's not far off . . .

It's interesting that the belief in Gog and Magog has, in the last war, taken on a reasonable, or rational, character. The belief that this war is the last has now spread through the entire world. Countless people feel that the world has today arrived at such a crisis, after which there has to be a complete change in human history. There's a feeling that Hitler has to be that villain, that wicked character in the drama of the world, after whose demise there must be a happy ending. Many people say that Hitler will have taught the world, once and for all, that might is not right and that people can't rule the world with power alone. Any powers who may think of invading weaker nations will have before them the example of Hitler and will not themselves be in any rush to start a war.

Scholarship has shown many times that every legend has a bit of truth, or at least a bit of logic. It appears that this is also the case with the legend of Gog and Magog. Human imagination has always suspected that before better times can begin, there will be a period of great cruelty and persecution. There's an aphorism for this too: "It's always darkest before dawn." The fact that Hitlerism has created such incomparable misery on the earth has stirred up the feeling in many people that we are dealing with a break in human history as a whole, with a darkness after which there must be light for a long time.

The tone and topic of this article cannot be dissociated from one of the most significant events in Singer's life during this period: the death of his older brother, Israel Joshua Singer, of a heart attack on February 10. The two brothers were not close at the time. In a letter dated 1938, written to his ex-lover Runia Pontsh in Palestine, Singer wrote, "My brother has become a great success here. Artistically, in my opinion, he has gone downhill." By the time of his brother's death, the two Singers led separate lives and pursued separate careers—as Singer had shown with the rerelease in 1943 of his novel *Satan in Goray*, which included four new stories written in the voice of the *Yeytser-hore*, the Evil Spirit. Still, his brother's death grieved and angered Singer in ways that perhaps he himself had not expected, especially as it came after the death of his mother and younger brother in Central Asia and the ongoing estrangement from his older sister, Esther Kreitman. When he writes, "Experience shows that every year, every single day, brings with it unforeseen losses that can never be replaced," he appears to speak not only of the millions of Jews annihilated in Eastern Europe but also of his brother, whose loss was both unforeseen and irreplaceable—not only for Singer but also for Yiddish literature, language, and culture as a whole.

The Yiddish That We Spoke in the Old Country Is Being Forgotten

(March 13, 1944)

For some time now, people have spoken of Yiddish and Hebrew coming closer together. It's also been shown several times in the *Forverts* that it's hard to understand what exactly this "closer together" is supposed to be about— or what we're supposed to do about it. You can't bring one language closer to another. Yiddish cannot form a united front with Hebrew. Each language has its history, its fate. There's a natural closeness between Hebrew and Yiddish. They are both Jewish languages. They influence each other. But these are things that happen *naturally*— we can't decide to increase their proximity.

But there is one realm in which Hebrew and Yiddish are coming closer together—one that is quite tragic.

Yiddish used to have—and still has—one major quality that Hebrew did not have until recently: it is a living language, one that does not necessarily have to be gleaned from books but that can be learned from people's mouths. The Hebraists had to resurrect Hebrew, while the Yiddishists were working with a living language. The Hebraists had to find words in the Talmud, but Yiddish writers could, every single day, hear new words and expressions in the marketplace—from their parents, relatives, and friends. Yiddish writers were always proud of this fact, and their pride was justified. Thousands of old

75

books cannot take the place of a living source. Hebrew writers were always jealous of Yiddish writers for being able to draw their language directly from the people.

But there are signs that in the recent years the situation has considerably changed for the worse, and that there's a risk that Yiddish will indeed get closer to Hebrew—which is to say that it, too, will become a dead language, a language of books. This kind of coming together would not be a joyful event.

The reasons are as follows:

First, the destruction of Poland, where the Jews have been literally annihilated, has wiped away a rich folk culture and impoverished the treasures of Yiddish. With the loss of each Yiddish community, many customs, sayings, and words have also been lost. The loss of living people is, naturally, an incomparably greater tragedy than the cultural loss. But Hitler has also brought a spiritual catastrophe upon the Jews.

Second, Jews who live in other countries quickly forget the customs and traditions, often even the words and sayings, of the old country. American Jews no longer speak the Yiddish that their mothers and fathers spoke. It's completely natural for them to mix all kinds of English words and sayings into their Yiddish. They forget many things about the old way of life. Time does the rest. Changes in circumstances change their language and their habits. You meet Jews in America who have only been in the country a few years but have managed to forget so much that it would seem they've been here for decades. The average person on the street is not interested in remembering useless, impractical things and forgets them with astounding speed . . .

Third, the majority of Jewish children—nearly *all* Jewish children—are not raised in Yiddish, and there's a risk that, very soon, Yiddish writers will no longer have living sources on which to draw. Just as Hebraists look for words in the Talmud, or just try borrowing words from Arabic, so will those who want to write in Yiddish have to look for words in Yiddish books. We're not talking about a time when Yiddish goes completely extinct. We're talking about a time when the Yiddish press still exists. There will still be Yiddish readers. But the living Yiddish language will have changed so much, will have been so Anglicized or Hispanicized, that when someone wants to write about the old country and use the language of that time there will no longer be anywhere to draw it from.

Our mothers and fathers are dying. Many of them manage to forget their Yiddish even before they die. There are no immigrants coming from the old country. Those who may yet come will obviously be in such shock that there will be little to learn from them. This period is comparable to the destruction of the Second Temple. Our enemies decimated the Jews along with their language. If the Hebrew Bible had been lost then—and it could have certainly happened—almost nothing would have been left of Hebrew. And without the Bible, there would obviously have been no Talmud either.

I'm saying this in response to those who mock Yiddish writers. Yiddish cultural producers today have a mission, which is not to let our cultural treasures be lost. As long as Jews from the older generation are still alive, as long as there still exists a living source, we have to make use of it. We have to begin producing—while there's still time—a comprehensive Yiddish dictionary. We must record all the customs of all the Jewish cities and shtetls. We must collect all kinds of sayings and proverbs. A source must be prepared for future Yiddish writers and historians—which, if it won't be living, will at least be rich. We must stress the urgency with which this mission needs to be accomplished. Experience shows that every year, every single day, brings with it unforeseen losses that can never be replaced. There are times when haste is not a vice but a virtue . . .

There actually exists an institution that should take this mission upon itself. This is the YIVO Institute for Jewish Research. But this very organization has not yet exhibited the energy and initiative—or really a full understanding of the situation. YIVO has not turned into an organization that can, with the greatest energy and haste, compile our people's inheritance. They do their work slowly, dragging along. YIVO's leadership, it seems, doesn't have the sense that every day that passes is another day wasted. They don't have the sense that there's a fire raging—and that we have to quickly pack up our dearest possessions. They act as if everything were peaceful and quiet.

YIVO has for years collected important material in Poland, in Ukraine, in Lithuania—but its leadership didn't grasp that Vilna was not a secure location. Hitler had already sharpened his teeth on Poland. Everyone predicted the Nazis could, any day, march into Lithuania. YIVO's leadership should have hired a ship and sent all the material they'd collected to America. But they did not do this—and it has all, most likely, been destroyed. These destroyed treasures can never be collected again. It's a good thing to stay calm and collected—but there are also moments when distress is just as important. YIVO's leadership stayed calm while the roof was already burning. This kind of calm is difficult to forgive.

Some of YIVO's leadership later came to America and started over. But they continue to exhibit a calm that smacks of indifference. They don't feel like each passing day is important. Instead of doing the hard work, they occupy themselves with trivialities or with things that can be set aside for later. This way, they miss what's most important.

YIVO is publishing, for example, a history of the Jewish Labor Movement in America. This is not an urgent undertaking. The material will not be lost. But work on a comprehensive Yiddish dictionary is put off year after year . . . In the journals that YIVO publishes, you encounter expressions and assertions about the Yiddish language that elicit shock in Yiddish writers. One day, the writer of these very lines came upon an invitation to lectures about "ancient" Yiddish and "primitive" Yiddish. This writer did not know whether to laugh or cry. What is "ancient" Yiddish anyway? And what is "primitive" Yiddish? The Yiddish that was spoken by our fathers and mothers, our grandfathers and grandmothers, is disappearing before our eyes—it's being lost—and here they play around with academic terms? This would have been the right thing to do were Yiddish in the same situation as English or Spanish. Under normal circumstances, one could afford such intellectual luxuries. No one would be any poorer if a philologist from YIVO discovered that this word belonged to ancient Yiddish while another belonged to primitive Yiddish. Every nation has its philologists. We should have ours too. But we can't afford it!

The situation is such that a number of Yiddish writers will have to take the work onto their own weak shoulders. Haim Nahman Bialik, the Hebrew poet, has in a certain sense—all on his own—started the work of collecting Hebrew linguistic and cultural treasures. He did this not because he believed that this is the task of the poet. It would have been better for Bialik the poet if he could occupy himself only with his poetry. But he felt that there weren't any others who would take the issue seriously.

Our situation is much more serious and much worse. Yiddish writers, journalists, and playwrights should make contact with knowledgeable representatives of all the *landsmanshaftn*—the hometown societies—in America and obtain from them the words and sayings that were used in their shtetls . . .

It would be a great thing for the Hebrew language if more Hebrew texts were found—even if they were in bits and fragments. A time may come when Yiddish scholars are in the same situation, and they'll ask: Why didn't people collect enough material when they saw that the sources were drying up? Why did they leave material sitting around that could have been published? What were they waiting for—these one-time Yiddish patriots? How did they justify feeling so relaxed, so calm, when they found themselves in the midst of catastrophes and ruins?

Like the previous article, this one is saturated with personal sentiment, as Singer later noted in his memoirs that he was exposed to the tales of Rabbi Nahman by his younger brother Moyshe, the only Singer sibling to have remained strictly religious. After their father died in 1929, Moyshe took over his father's rabbinate in Stary Dzików, a small Galician town near modern-day Lviv, where he also cared for their mother. In 1939 the two were deported to Jambyl, Kazakhstan, from which they sent postcards and radiograms through the first years of World War II. The last radiogram to be found in Singer's archives, dated January 21, 1942, reads: *"MONEY PACKAGE DRESSING SEND MOSES SINGER MOTHER ILL."* After this, nothing appears to have been heard from them. The publication of an article about Rabbi Nahman two months after Israel Joshua's death may reflect Singer's return to the textual sources that gave him spiritual strength, connecting to his family legacy, and were also, for him, closely tied to questions of faith and doubt, with which he struggled his whole life. Indeed, the previous time Singer had written about Rabbi Nahman was in December 1939 and January 1940, just weeks after the outbreak of World War II and the deportation of his brother and mother to the USSR. For Singer, it seems, the question of faith and doubt was tied up with his brother, who represented his father's religious lineage, as well as with Rabbi Nahman, whose tales offered an original form of Yiddish folkloric storytelling that also lived up to Singer's literary, aesthetic criteria—and that represented, for him, a path forward in Yiddish literature.

Rabbi Nahman Told Stories that Delighted Our Grandparents

(April 2, 1944)

Of all Yiddish storytellers, the most talented was surely Rabbi Nahman of Bratslav. Rabbi Nahman was, above all, an interesting person. His own life story sounds like a tale from a storybook.

Rabbi Nahman of Bratslav was the grandson of the Baal Shem Tov, who, as many know, was the founder of Hasidism and the first great rebbe—Hasidic leader. Thousands of stories and miracles are told about the Baal Shem. A whole body of literature was written about him.

The Baal Shem had a daughter named Hodl. There are many legends about this daughter. It is told that in moments of great religious ecstasy, she danced together with the Hasidim, and even though it is obviously considered a sin for men to dance with women, an exception was made for Hodl. She was the Baal Shem's daughter, and no one could suspect her of dancing with men because of sinful desires. No, she did it out of love for God, out of holy ecstasy. So say Hasidim.

Hodl had two sons who played a large role in the Hasidic world, and one daughter, Feige, also called Feigele. Feigele married the son of Rabbi Nahman of Horodenka, one of the Baal Shem's disciples. When she got pregnant and had a son, she named him after his grandfather, Rabbi Nahman of Horodenka.

This child, who was the grandchild of both the Baal Shem and of Rabbi Nahman of Horodenka, was, from the cradle, raised to be a rebbe. People expected great things from a lineage like his, and they were not fooling themselves. Nahman grew into a powerful personality in the Hasidic world.

It's said that, while he was still in the cradle, a yarmulke was put on his head, and a *tallis-kotn*—a fringed undershirt—on his body. He began talking early, before he left the cradle, and he was taught to say a blessing over the milk he suckled from his mother's breast. We can't say whether this is true. But it could have been true.

When Nahman was six years old, he fasted on a regular basis so that God would forgive him his sins, though it's hard to say what sins he could have committed. He studied Torah day and night and demonstrated a level of knowledge that amazed people. Nahman belonged to that class of geniuses who mature early.

At the age of thirteen, he was married off. His father-in-law leased an estate near a village, and Nahman spent the first years after his wedding among fields and forests. He liked going into the forest and praying among the trees. He regularly took long walks through the fields. Nahman had a poetic soul. He loved beauty and had a rich imagination that carried him off into fantastic worlds. He became a rebbe while still young and acquired many fervent followers. Rabbi Nahman belonged to that class of people that were either extremely loved or extremely hated. Many rabbis, religious youth, and Hasidim said that he had surpassed his grandfather, the Baal Shem, and that he was even one of the very greatest people that the world had ever seen. Conversely, others maintained that he exaggerated everything—that he was a showoff and also half crazy. He had bitter enemies who slandered him and nearly had him excommunicated. Rabbi Nahman would say about his enemies that they hated not him but someone else, a man they had invented, since he believed that they did not actually know him personally. The man they hated was not him, Rabbi Nahman.

All rebbes taught Torah during communal meals. But Rabbi Nahman's teaching was so full of imagination, so interesting, so deep and poetic, that it can barely be compared to the teaching of other rebbes. His teachings even make an impression on unbelievers who read his religious books today. His teachings interweave a bit of poetry, deep psychological observations, and very often also a bit of philosophy. Aside from teaching Torah, Rabbi Nahman also liked telling stories. Rabbi Nahman had the temperament of a poet and a romantic nature. He drew his tales from his frighteningly rich imagination. Every one of his stories was a parable. Hasidim have said that behind every one of his words, great and sublime secrets lie hidden. But the stories themselves were extremely interesting in their own right.

Rabbi Nahman believed that a righteous *tzaddik*, a rebbe, could only reach his highest level of spirituality in the Land of Israel. He spoke many times with his disciples about there being numerous secrets that he could not attain because he was "abroad," that is, outside of the Land of Israel. On one Friday, after the mikvah, Rabbi Nahman let his disciples know that he had decided on making the journey to the Land of Israel. He *had* to go! No one could stop him!

Rabbi Nahman was then around twenty-six or twenty-seven years old, but he already had a marriageable daughter, and she started wailing when she heard that her father was going away. His wife, the rebbetzin, cried bitterly too. In those days, a trip to the Land of Israel involved many dangers. The journey itself took an entire year. There is a chronicle of this journey. It is the most fantastic story of Hasidic life. Rabbi Nahman risked his life dozens of times. He was taken prisoner. He traveled on a warship. He had all kinds of adventures in Constantinople. There are facts showing that the trip had shaken Rabbi Nahman so much that for some time he was not in his right mind. In Constantinople, for example, he began playing with children and did other strange things.

Like many other romantic poets, Rabbi Nahman was the kind of person who often found himself on the border between sanity and insanity. His religious fervor often carried him off to a world that had nothing in common with the practical world. This doesn't mean that Rabbi Nahman was a mentally disturbed person. We have to remember that many great poets had times when they were on the verge of insanity . . .

Rabbi Nahman did not himself set his stories in writing. He told them orally. But one of his most devoted disciples, Reb Noson, wrote them down word for word and later published them. Reb Noson also wrote the biography of his rebbe, Rabbi Nahman, the story of his life, where he portrays him as a divine man. One cannot imagine a greater admiration than the kind that Reb Noson had for Rabbi Nahman . . .

It doesn't matter how you interpret Rabbi Nahman's tales, but they are all open for interpretation—and each one is profound. The marvelous tales that Rabbi Nahman of Bratslav told came from a great poet and represent the highest achievement of literary storytelling. He gave his readers a beautiful story, deep meaning, an interesting parable, and profound moral insight.

This article represents Singer's treatment of contemporary political debates about a Jewish national home, which had raged before, during, and after World War II. It was Singer's second article on the topic in a matter of weeks, the first being "All Jews in Palestine Support a Jewish State" (March 20, 1944), which talks about the difference between a Jewish commonwealth and a binational state—one of the major questions being debated then. This article was published during the Biltmore Conference taking place in New York at the Biltmore Hotel May 6-11—a time when, because of the war, it was impossible to hold the annual Zionist Congress because of the war. Preparing policies for Jewish self-determination after the defeat of the Nazi Germany, the conference ended with a declaration that "that the new world order that will follow victory cannot be established on foundations of peace, justice and equality, unless the problem of Jewish homelessness is finally solved." Singer's article addresses not only the issue of a Jewish national home but also the history of Jews as a disenfranchised nation that has internalized powerlessness as an existential condition—which sets the stage for a drive for power.

Is Being Powerless a Jewish Ideal?

(May 8, 1944)

When we read Jewish history, we see—in every generation, in every epoch—the same picture: a Jewish settlement is established, Jews build up the land, do business,
found yeshivas, turn out rabbis and scholars. All at once,
a band of murderers falls upon the settlement. Jewish
women and children are killed. Our rabbis and community leaders are dragged through the mud. Vile thugs,
drunks, and brutes stomp their feet on everything that is
dear and holy to us, and————

From many we become few, and these few flee in
every possible direction. We have new *kedoshim*, martyrs,
new penitential prayers are composed, and lamentations
over the new destruction. And this is how it is, one generation after another.

In these lamentations, these *kinot*, Jews plead with
God: "Look down and see our disgrace. We are like
sheep led to slaughter. How long, God? How long? How
long?"

Every new destruction has led to the composition
of new *kinot* and *selichot*, penitential prayers. Old-time
prayer books were very thick. People had to recite *selichot*
almost every day. But many *kinot* and *selihot* have been
forgotten. We've had too many *kedoshim*, too many misfortunes, for them all to be remembered.

When we open a bookcase full of religious books

and gaze upon our old books of wisdom, with their leather covers and gold embossing, we often forget that a considerable number of the authors who wrote these books of ours had been slaughtered, beaten, or driven away. Any drunk or scoundrel was capable of offending and torturing our spiritual leaders. From time to time, students would hunt down Jews just like helpless animals are hunted. These hunts were known in our sad history as "schoolboy stampedes."

These religious Jews had one hope: that the Godhead would sooner or later have mercy on its chosen people and redeem them, taking revenge on the spilled blood of its servants. Without this very hope, our forebears would not have been able to exist. When the Jews of old let themselves be led to the slaughter like sheep, they did so with the belief that, as soon as they were slaughtered, their souls would enter the Garden of Eden. Whereas the souls of their murderers would suffer in Gehenna forever. This endowed their powerlessness with some meaning.

Modern Jews don't possess this kind of belief. They know that if someone kills them, they're dead, and that murderers very often have plenty of ways to avoid punishment. The world is full of murderers who eat and drink and who even act like great heroes. Jew killers are the least punished of all murderers. Their number is too great. There was no way to punish all those who took part in pogroms in Ukraine, in Poland, and in Belarus just twenty or so years ago. And who will even bother locating every boor, every scoundrel, who has tortured the Jews during the current destruction? Entire peoples have taken part in these slaughters.

Modern Jews know—if they are thinking people—that powerlessness is nothing to be proud of, nothing to brag about. Nature is built in such a way that the weak perish and the strong remain after them. Lions, tigers, and wolves devour lambs, hares, and rabbits, and they are not punished for it, though the lambs are completely innocent. We too eat the flesh of poor chickens, sheep, and calves, our only justification being that we are stronger. We sometimes give a sigh over the fate of the poor chicken or the helpless calf. But then we immediately order ourselves a steak.

Yes—the weak are miserable! Wretched and miserable! There is no comfort in powerlessness. No comfort, at least, of which we know.

Every nation strives to be strong. Every class wants power. When the working class became conscious of how wretched their situation was it strove for power, and with good reason. Because what good would all of their laments have brought had they remained helpless? Unions, political parties—they were all created to strengthen the workers' hand.

We are saying this in response to a number of modern writers—people who do not live religious lifestyles—who have recently begun praising our powerlessness. In *Ghetto in Flames*, a collection that includes several descriptions of true Jewish heroism, we also find a sentence that reads:

It was a battle for the honor of powerlessness, and it may have even surpassed the battles of the Maccabees in the destruction of Jerusalem. *Powerlessness* now raised its flags and was exulted with fanfare. The great and eternal *Jewish* battle was the battle for the importance of powerlessness.

A little later, it says:

> The heroism of world powerlessness is the heroism of Jewish history.

If words have any sort of meaning, and there is responsibility behind them, the question begs to be asked: Why are modern Jews such great supporters of powerlessness? What so-called joys has powerlessness brought us? Why should powerlessness "raise its flags" and "be exulted with fanfare"? All in all, because of our powerlessness we have lost our nearest and dearest. Our dignity has been trampled by dirty feet. Had we not been so powerless, so defenseless, the Nazis could not have with complete impunity led millions of Jews to the slaughter like sheep.

When we read about the battles in the ghettos we are filled with pride, but we ask ourselves: Why were there so few fighters? Why had they waited so long? And we know that the fault lies not only with our physical but also with our psychological powerlessness—the fact that we were brought up for generations to be sheep and to die like sheep. If, for our parents, powerlessness had some justification or rationale, for us it is little more than a tragedy and a disgrace. There's nothing to brag about. It's a condition against which we have to fight with all our might . . .

No human group has been brought up to be as completely helpless and sheeplike as Jews. A single thug was able to instill fear in an entire town. A single drunk could often unleash a pogrom. The only Jews who didn't let others take advantage of them were the uneducated workers. The butchers and wagon drivers were not ashamed to carry knives, to brandish sticks or iron rods, and they actually commanded some respect. If not for them, the shtetls would have seen pogroms every day.

This piece was a response to an article published in February 1944 by the *Contemporary Jewish Record*—soon thereafter relaunched as *Commentary*—in which young Jewish intellectuals under forty answered questions about the relationship, in their eyes, between American literature and American Jewish identity. Among the interviewees were Clement Greenberg, Alfred Kazin, Muriel Rukeyser, Delmore Schwartz, and Lionel Trilling. As with "The Yiddish That We Spoke in the Old World Is Being Forgotten," published two months earlier, so the angry tone of this article cannot be dissociated from the loss of Singer's brother, Israel Joshua, who for him was not only a great writer but also highly knowledgeable as a Jew. This article also demonstrates the gap that existed between American Jewish culture and the culture of the "old country" where Singer grew up—a gap that he eventually exploited using his public persona as an old-fashioned storyteller. At this point, however, Singer's view into American Jewish life was like a two-way mirror: he could see into the lives of American Jewish intellectuals, but those same intellectuals had no way of knowing anything about his life or work. A large part of Singer's later career involved creating pathways linking these two sides. In this article, he is working through the nature of his relationship to American Jews and reaches his first major insight: American Jews need to feel that they can gain more from their Jewish identities than just gloom and doom. They need access to a fire that will keep them spiritually alive. With time, in addition to his literary and aesthetic concerns, Singer came to structure much of his work around this need for spiritual fire.

Does Being Jewish Influence the Work of Jews Who Are American Writers?

(May 22, 1944)

The editor of a Yiddish newspaper in Warsaw gave a job to a young journalist. Then he told him: If you're ever lacking for a topic to write about, you should think about three sorts of topics that will come in handy anytime you need.

The first topic: *Is a given non-Jew a friend or an enemy of the Jews?*

The second topic: *Is a given famous Jew connected to the Jewish people or not?*

The third topic consists of taking the Jewish question and attaching it to some unrelated issue. For example, winter and the Jewish question, or love and the Jewish question. The moon and the Jewish question. There's nothing in the world that can't be combined with the Jewish question.

So if you remember these rules, you won't die of hunger for lack of topics to write about.

The English-language Jewish magazine *The Jewish Record*, which is published by the American Jewish Committee, has recently made an inquiry among a number of writers of Jewish descent. The question was: How does your Jewish descent—your Jewish heritage—influence your writing? In their work, are these writers actively conscious of being Jewish, or does being Jewish play an unconscious, passive role in their writing? The inquiry was made among writers who were under forty years old. The editors had probably believed that younger people would be more honest. Old writers are old diplomats.

So far, eleven writers have answered. You can't say that the answers aren't honest. They've all made an effort to say what they think about the issue. But what comes out is a stutter of sorts—the words of people who are terribly embarrassed and who've just had their weakest point pressed. When you read these writers' answers, you get the impression that they were all angry at being asked such a question. It appears that modern Jews, just like Christians, don't like it very much when you start interrogating them about how much love they have for the Jewish people and for Judaism. As it says in the *Song of Songs*: better not to awaken love and tear it to pieces. Better to let it ripen on its own.

Why does this question elicit such embarrassment?

The answer is: How *couldn't* it elicit embarrassment?

These writers are not religious Jews. Their language is English. They know only a little Yiddish. Being Jewish is a problem for them from beginning to end. They're all proud of being Jewish and are all sworn enemies of Hitler. But that's about it. When you take such people and start examining their Jewishness, they're overcome with anxiety. You've opened up the wound known as being a modern Jew.

Modern Jews in America suffer on account of being Jewish. They feel that they are victims at every turn. But they don't know what they're suffering for. What does Judaism give them? What does it consist of? Where is it taking them? What has it taught them, and what legacy can they pass on to their children? Somewhere, deep in their hearts, many modern Jews feel that being Jewish is a bit of bad luck and nothing else. Even those who have made peace with their fate don't like to talk about it.

This is the feeling you get when you read their answers. The fault does not lie with the writers. The fault lies with the situation.

Jews were meant to be a nation, to have their own land, to speak their own language, and to serve their own God. When Jews have their God, their land, their language, and their nationality all torn away, they're left with nothing but their origins, their race, and no one wants to suffer for their race. Somewhere in these modern Jews there's a rebellion, an aversion to the whole thing. You feel it even when they praise Judaism. But not everyone has praise. Many of them have bitter words. The answers aren't as characteristic for writers in particular as they are for young Jews in general. What they say is the same thing that's said by all of our children who haven't gotten a proper Jewish education . . .

You can't say that these young American writers are ashamed of being Jewish, or that they hate it, or that they are assimilationists. No, in America, the type of assimilation that aims to imitate Christians—to win their favor and to disregard those Jews who still conduct their lives in Yiddish—is not yet popular. This ugly phenomenon is not characteristic for America. Young American Jews are proud people. If they say that Jewish heritage is unfamiliar to them, it's because that's the case. These writers don't know much about either the old Jewish sources or the new ones. They haven't had the chance to connect to Judaism as much as Yiddish or Hebrew writers. They've been raised on a Judaism without vitality, without clearly defined ideals, without direction. What they get from this kind of Judaism is nearly worthless—but what they have to pay for it carries a high price. This kind of situation cannot but elicit bitterness.

The writers discussed here have still had at least a taste of Yiddishkayt. Their answers suggest that some of them can speak a little Yiddish. Others studied at a Hebrew Sunday school. These writers' children—or, put a better way, our children's children—will most probably not have even this sort of Jewish education. A generation of Jews is growing up in America knowing less about Jews than the average Christian. They've heard something about there having been pogroms in Russia, they read about Hitler's persecution of the Jews in the newspapers, and on the street they meet refugees who speak German or who escaped the concentration camps. That's all. For the sake of this dreary Jewishness—which has nothing positive, no real values—these same young people have to endure both open and hidden oppression. On account of this "Jewishness," they have to deal with difficulties finding a job, getting into college, finding a summer home, and all kinds of other hardships.

There are institutions in America that are trying to do something about this issue. There are Yiddish and Hebrew schools. But the number of children who study there is small, and the amount of Jewish knowledge and fire that they find there is even smaller.

If in the old world, we, like our parents, suffered

physically, a Jewish generation is now growing up in America that will be completely lost spiritually. The Jewishness that they take on will be a burden and nothing else. It shouldn't surprise anyone if many of them try with all their strength to cast this burden off. At least if anyone lets them.

The moral, in the broadest sense of the word, is that Jewishness that's not connected to the old sources, with their ancient aspirations and ideals, cannot spiritually maintain Jews as a minority. Those groups interested in the survival of Yiddishkayt must rebuild their educational systems. They have to give children the ability to know as much as possible about all aspects of Jewish life. A smattering of Yiddishkayt doesn't have enough fire to spiritually sustain Jews in the cold atmosphere being created around them.

Singer's realization in the previous article—that American Jews need to have the past linked directly to the present—offers good context for how this article is framed: linking the Allied liberation of France, a current event of great interest to Jews in the United States, to the pre- and early-medieval history of Jews in Europe, about which they likely know little. It also reveals an implicit understanding that Yiddish-speaking American Jews could be as lacking in knowledge of Jewish history as English-speaking Jews—that as graduates of secular school systems, they too needed to be informed of the Jewish connection between historical and current events. This explains, in part, how Singer's stories functioned, in cultural terms, in both Yiddish and English—they spoke to readers who were, at their core, culturally American. Singer is slowly developing an understanding of his most immediate readership—American Jews—already in the Yiddish language. The transition he makes to English later in his life is not as radical as has been assumed by many critics. In both Yiddish and English, Singer speaks to readers who are interested in Jewish history and culture without having a great deal of knowledge, searching for access to its riches.

Pages Out of Jewish History from French Cities the American Army Is Now Liberating

(June 18, 1944)

During the current invasion of France, we find ourselves reading about very many cities and towns that sound strange to our ears. But this doesn't mean that our great-grandfathers and great-grandmothers didn't once live in these very towns. Many French Jews migrated in different periods from France to settle in Germany and later in Poland and Russia. There are a number of French words that made their way into Yiddish. All Jews follow rules that were established by rabbis in France. Rashi and the Tosafot, which every religious Jewish boy learned in heder and in the study house, all came from France. Whenever we recited our penitential prayers during the Days of Awe, or when we recited parts of our prayer books during Rosh Hashanah or Yom Kippur, we most probably didn't know that these religious words were actually composed in faraway France.

Jews have lived in France since the country was a colony of the Roman Empire. Documents exist from the fifth century that mention Jews in France, or Gaul, as it was then called . . . When the Romans occupied nearby France, Jewish merchants from Rome began making trips there. The Jews of Rome brought Jewish and Roman culture to France. Jews taught those who lived in France at the time to speak Latin, the language from which

French later developed. Slowly, the Roman Empire collapsed, and France came to be ruled by three tribes: the Visigoths, the Burgundians, and the Franks. But before completely splitting off from Rome, the French adopted Christianity.

There is a document from 425 CE where Jews are forbidden from being lawyers or government officials. In the year 465 CE, a conference of priests forbade the clergy to eat with Jews. The thinking was that since Jews would not eat with Christians, whose food was unkosher, the priests would not eat with Jews.

Documents from the sixth century show that Jews were already living in Marseilles, in Orléans, in Paris, in Bordeaux, and in a number of other cities and regions. They already had their own schools and study houses, where they also prayed. Jews were occupied with trade and with tax collection. They were also doctors and had ships that brought merchandise to local ports. Many French people converted to Judaism during this time. A document from 538 CE forbade matches between Jews and Christians. This shows that there were already mixed marriages in France at the time. But it appears that French women were taking on Jewish ways of life. The same document says that when Jews convert someone French, the Jews have to be punished by losing their slaves. It was also forbidden for Jews to be judges and to have Christian slaves. At the time, there were still plenty of pagans living in France. In 576 CE, a synagogue had already been set on fire in France. In 582 CE, there was a fight between a Jew by the name of Priscus and a Jewish apostate named Fatir. The apostate murdered the Jew, and the Jew's relatives took revenge and killed the apostate. There are documents showing that during the eighth century, Jews lived in the part of France called Provence, where they had farms and vineyards.

When Charlemagne, or Charles the Great, became king of France in 768 CE, he showed much friendship toward the Jews. At that time, in a certain region, the Jews had a "ruler" of their own, a kind of Jewish king. There are documents showing this, and it's also mentioned by Rabbi Meir of Narbonne, son of Rabbi Shimon, in his religious book *Milhemet Mitsva*, or *Holy War*. Charlemagne had invited a Jewish spiritual leader from Babylon, Rabbi Makhir, who was descended from King David. Rabbi Makhir held the title of "president," which was as good as "prince." Rabbi Makhir's son and grandson were also presidents for the Jews. During this time, Jews were even appointed as diplomats in the French government. Jews served as royal doctors and took other high positions.

One of the most famous and brilliant Jewish scholars in France was Rabbeinu Gershom "Meor HaGola"—the Light of the Exile. It was Rabbeinu Gershom who established the rule that Jews must not take more than one wife. It appears that until then rich Jews still took several wives. There are many legends about how this rule came about. Rabbeinu Gershom was supposed to have had two wives himself, and one of them had supposedly betrayed him horribly, leading him to be imprisoned in a tower, where he was supposed to die of hunger. But Rabbeinu Gershom got out using his wisdom, and the treacherous wife died. We can't say how much of all this is true. But Rabbeinu Gershom did institute a second rule: that a woman can't be forced to divorce. If a woman does not want to divorce, she can't be compelled to do so . . .

The most famous of all of the great scholars and Torah commentators that France produced was Rashi. The word *Rashi* is an acronym for *Ra*bbi *Sh*lomo *I*tzkhaki. Rashi was born in 1040 CE in Troyes, which was then the capital of the Champagne region. When he was young, Rashi studied in different yeshivas. At the time, the *Hakhmei Lothar*, the sages of Lotharingia, were especially well known. Rashi studied in their yeshivas, which were then located on both sides of the Rhine River. His most important teacher was Rabbi Yaakov ben Yakir. When he was done studying in these yeshivas, he returned to Troyes, where he began to compose his famous commentaries, his *perush* or interpretation of the Talmud and of the Hebrew Bible. No one knows if each of the Rashi commentaries for each paragraph truly originates with Rashi. There are different opinions about this. But he surely wrote commentaries on both the Talmud and the Five Books of Moses. Rashi's talents as an interpreter, as a Talmud commentator, were extraordinary.

There are many reasons why studying Talmud without commentaries is difficult. First, the Talmud is written in a mix of Hebrew and Aramaic. When the Talmud was written, Jews in Babylon spoke a kind of "Yiddish" that mixed these two languages. Jews of other lands and later generations no longer understood Aramaic, which made studying Talmud very difficult. Second, the writing in the Talmud is very condensed. A single word can sometimes contain the meaning of an entire sentence. Without an interpretation, people can't usually understand the slightest bit of Gemara. Rashi translated everything. And in so doing Rashi himself didn't say too much either . . . Very often, when Rashi wanted to explain an unfamiliar word, he translated it into French. But at that time people did not speak today's French. They spoke Old French.

In both his time and long after, Rashi held the greatest level of recognition. Even the most incisive Jewish scholars, those who criticized everyone, praised Rashi to the skies. Rabbeinu Abraham ben David, known as the Rabad, who had bitterly torn Maimonides to pieces, thought the world of Rashi. In his book *Sefer HaKabbalah* he wrote, "A great light has appeared in France, of a kind the eyes have never seen. This is our great teacher, Rabbi Shlomo of Troyes . . . If ever, God forbid, the Torah has been forgotten among the Jews, he has made it so that it will never be forgotten."

The famous biblical scholar and poet Rabbi Abraham Ibn Ezra wrote Rashi a song of praise. Jews had a saying: *Rashi isn't crazy*. This kind of talk, which made light of Rashi, was not at all an expression of disdain but rather of love. Scholars gave Rashi the nickname Parshandata, who was one of Haman's sons, and such a name would normally have been an insult to Rashi. But this too was an expression of love. Since Rashi was indeed a *parshan*, an interpreter, they gave him this name. No other Jewish genius has ever been given a nickname.

Rashi raised his children in the same spirit as he lived. His daughter was a famous scholar. His son-in-law, Rabbi Meir ben Samuel of Ramerupt, took part in writing the Tosafot, as did one of Rashi's students, Rabbi Itzkhak ben Asher, known as the Riba. And two of Rashi's grandsons, the Rashbam and Rabbeinu Tam, both achieved great fame. They were brothers, and they were both brilliant scholars . . .

This was how great Jewish figures created a Jewish culture of their own in the France of that time. Many generations have passed, and now, in those cities where our rabbis, poets, and geniuses lived, Hitler's Nazis and his French henchmen are running rampant. The Allied armies now have to liberate these same cities from the fascist trash.

We have no room here to give a picture of all of Jewish history in France. But we can put it in a few words: we built, and our enemies destroyed. Crusades, expulsions, blood libels, and bitter decrees led to the destruction of Jewish life. As soon as we recovered from one blow, another one soon came. From the earliest decrees against the Jews to the Dreyfus Affair and the Vichy laws runs one long chain of persecution. As soon as we were left alone for even a moment, we prospered both economically and spiritually. But these periods of rest were short. Out of almost two thousand years of history in France, we are left with little but pages from religious books.

This article is one of many in which Singer treats the topic of what he refers to as the "Modern Jew." Others from this time period include "They're Not Religious but They Yearn for Shabbat and for Jewish Holidays" (October 21, 1943), "Jews Who Call Themselves Religious but Aren't Observant" (April 3, 1944), "The Modern Jew Grows Increasingly into a General Problematic" (October 9, 1944), and "For Them Judaism Is a Mystery" (July 2, 1945). This article was chosen because of its focus on Yiddishkayt in both cultural and religious terms, as well as the historical contextualization of Jews who rejected Judaism while knowing something about it, and Jews who are proud of being Jewish but don't know what it means—or how to make it meaningful. Within the volume, this article is the one in which the Yiddish word *yidishkayt* has been translated with the greatest degree of variation.

They Don't Know Why They're Jewish, But They Don't Want to Be Anything Else

(June 26, 1944)

A new sort of Jew has appeared in recent years—a type that has never before existed in Jewish history. These Jews are not ashamed of being Jewish, don't change their Jewish names, will never pretend to be anything else, but at the same time don't actually know why they're Jewish, what Yiddishkayt means, or what they're supposed to do with it. For them, the whole issue of Jewishness is a problem from beginning to end.

Jewish history has had its share of apostates, unbelievers, false messiahs like Sabbatai Zevi and Jacob Frank, Karaites, and all kinds of sects. But never have there been Jews for whom the whole issue has itself been unfamiliar.

The unbelievers of olden days were Jews who knew how to study traditional Jewish texts. They could deny that the Torah came from the heavens, but their whole education was bound up with Jews and Judaism. The Karaites knew nothing of the Talmud, and so our type of Jews considered them heretics. But the Karaites had some relationship to Judaism. They wrote books, had their own Hebrew schools, their own *Shulhan Arukh*. Many Sabbateans believed that through sinning they will bring about the coming of the Messiah, which is why they sinned and did all kinds of other abominable things. But despite all this, Sabbateans were, in their own way, consciously Jewish. Between one transgression and another, they sat in the study house and learned Gemara. The Jews connected to the labor movement are not religious, but they speak Yiddish, they belong to Jewish organizations, they have specific ideas about Jews and Yiddishkayt. Even the former assimilationists of the old country had a Jewish program. They called themselves Russians, Poles, or Germans of the Mosaic faith. They went to synagogue, they established Jewish philanthropic institutions. They also had their own thoughts about how other Jews should conduct themselves. Their idea was that Jews in all countries should be loyal citizens, speak the local language, adapt themselves to the local lifestyle, and only maintain their religion, or a reformed version of their religion. Others had a downright negative relationship to Judaism. They were ashamed of being Jewish and wanted to escape from it.

But recent years have introduced, especially in America, a new type of Jew: one who knows nothing about Yiddishkayt. These Jews don't deny that they're Jewish, but they have no idea what it is, what obligations it brings to bear on them, and where it's taking them. They aren't religious and can't even go to synagogue to pray to God, in whom they don't believe. They speak no Yiddish. They weren't taught any Hebrew. They have no interest in Palestine, in the labor movement, or in any other such things. They're American, like all Americans, and are interested only in those things that are connected with life in this place. They've heard something about how, in the old country, grandma and grandpa used to be religious, but why should they be thinking of grandma and grandpa at all? Why should they be interested in a life that is totally unfamiliar to them?

But at the same time, they're Jewish. Their last names are Goldberg or Rosenbaum. They can't get jobs in certain fields and industries where Jews aren't accepted. If they want to go to a hotel, they have to make sure it's a hotel that allows Jews and not one that's for "Gentiles only." All of the libels that antisemites invent about Jews are directed at them too. They sometimes get a chance to say that they're proud of being Jewish, but at the same time they have no idea why they should actually be so proud. What constitutes their Yiddishkayt? And what will constitute their children's Yiddishkayt?

You hear interesting observations about Jews and Judaism from young people like these. A young man from New York noted that there are three types of Jews: those who live on the East Side, those who live in Brooklyn or the Bronx, and those who live on Central Park West and Park Avenue. This is actually all he knows about his people. Some of them will tell you that when they had their bar or bat mitzvah they prepared a "speech" of sorts but that they forgot it long ago. There is a frightening ignorance of Judaism presiding over the Jewish youth of America.

Four types of children are listed in the Passover Haggadah: smart ones, evil ones, simple ones, and ones who are so unknowledgeable that they don't even ask any questions. They don't even know what to ask questions *about*. A big part of American-born young men and women belong to this last type. They know so little about

Jews that they don't even ask anything. They've decided once and for all that for them being Jewish is a closed issue. For them being Jewish has become one of those things that's better not to talk about.

The circumstances that have led us to this situation are familiar to us all. The people who immigrated to America were young for the most part, children from poor families. Many of them had studied only a few years in heder and then soon went to work. There were those who, because of their poverty or because they were orphans, hadn't even really gone to heder. The little that they had learned in heder they soon forgot. Here in America they worked long and hard, barely having enough time to read the daily paper. Such parents could barely teach their children anything about Judaism. They told their children a little about the "old country," about their grandmas and grandpas. This was all there was. The children studied in American public schools, so it was natural for them to learn nothing about Judaism. A great number of Jewish lawyers, doctors, dentists, and teachers simply don't know the Hebrew alphabet. It's true that you can study Jewish history and gain Jewish knowledge in English. But to learn something you have to have an interest in it, and no one has instilled this interest in them. When lawyers or doctors like these try to learn something about Jewish history, they are soon bored. All of these tales of tribes and kings, temples and exiles—they all sound so foreign that they just toss the book aside.

What kind of Jewish generation will ensue from such parents? What will our grandchildren look like if our children are already so alienated?

This is a question that torments many Jewish people.

It can't be said that nothing is being done. There are Sunday schools, Hebrew schools, Yiddish schools, Talmud Torahs, yeshivas. Every party or group tries to solve the problem in its own way and according to its own viewpoints. But none of these institutions is having any great success. The number of children who study in Talmud Torahs and yeshivas, in Yiddish and Hebrew schools, is relatively small. Of those who do study there, a large percentage doesn't actually learn anything. A smattering of education is no education at all. You meet kids from Hebrew and Yiddish schools who can't actually speak Hebrew or Yiddish at all. The little they learn they soon forget. Naturally, it's better to know a little than nothing at all. There are no two minds about this. We have to recognize those who do all they can to give our younger generation a bit of Jewish knowledge. But we don't have to fool ourselves. The fruits of these labors are not great, and they are fruits that contain few seeds in them. There is little hope that from these kernels trees will grow . . .

This writer believes that a number of groups, which all work separately, could and should unite and create a common program and common methods. No approach has yet been developed that would get children *interested* in Jewish studies. Almost every teacher has their own personal methods. The right teachers' manual has not yet been published. We have not yet made the choices that need to be made. A great amount of professionalism and purpose is needed for educational institutions to get American children interested in Jewish knowledge. But in many cases the people who are drawn to this work are not prepared. Party affiliation and group patriotism also play a role.

Sure, the groups that have secular programs can't walk arm in arm with religious Jews who want to raise their kids strictly by the Torah. But secular Jews from different camps could easily come to an understanding.

This writer believes that both those who choose to ignore Yiddish literature and those who have the tendency to ignore both old and new Hebrew literature are committing an error. We can't raise our children on Yiddishism alone, but we also can't neglect everything that Jewish folk artists have created in Yiddish. Textbooks could be made that could include the core of both sources. In many cases, certain classes have to be conducted in English. A Yiddish teacher who can't speak English, or speaks it poorly, can rarely be successful with American-born children. The child can't respect the teacher if the child speaks the local language better and more fluently. The child will then look down at the teacher. In many cases the teachers are so overburdened and underpaid that they have no time or strength to fully devote themselves and to develop in their profession. Some of the teachers simply don't know their profession and are unsuited to it in every way.

These are questions that touch upon the foundation of our spiritual existence. We can't take them lightly and we can't put off solving them. There are children growing up now who know nothing about Yiddishkayt, and many of them already don't want to know anything about it at all.

Of all the types of Jews that have ever existed in our history, the most dangerous for our own existence are *indifferent* Jews. Such a generation is now growing up before our very eyes.

And considering how little we have done to prevent this, we ourselves may even be accused of indifference.

This article combines two perspectives on Jewish Warsaw that informed Singer's writing for the rest of his life: the perspective of a rabbi's son growing up on its side streets between 1907 and 1917, and the perspective of a young writer who moved back to the city of his childhood in 1923, living in different neighborhoods until he fled for New York in 1935. In some of his later writings, Singer differentiated between these two perspectives, but his work is always suffused with an ambiguity that blurs them together, as he does in this piece. It also represents Singer's focused efforts to memorialize an entire way of life—a mentality and perspective on life and on the world—encapsulated by Warsaw Jews.

Each Jewish Street in Warsaw Was Like a Town of Its Own

(July 2, 1944)

When people are struck by great misfortunes, by very powerful blows, they are in no condition to immediately take stock of what's happened to them. It can often take weeks, months, or even longer for people to be able to comprehend the scope of their tragedy.

The world's Jews are today living through this sort of thing. We've been struck such fearful blows that we've become partially numb to them. The horrible reports have reached us so quickly, one after another, that we've lost any sense of reality where this issue is concerned. The human mind can perhaps comprehend the cruelty of a single murder. But when it comes to mass murder, when we hear of thousands of children being buried alive, when we hear of places where hundreds of thousands of men, women, and children are being massacred, poisoned, burned to death—our imagination comes to a standstill. The nervous system can merely register such facts, but it can't respond to them. It's like someone saying that a star is a billion light-years away from us. We know that it's far, extremely far, but conceiving of such a distance is beyond our powers.

This is a little like our experience of reading about the number of Jewish victims. We are left standing paralyzed before an abyss.

The writer of these lines is a Warsaw native. He knows that there are no Jews left in Warsaw. But he can't properly conceive of the fact. When he uses the word *Warsaw*, he sees old Jewish Warsaw before him. He sees Jewish streets, shops, schools, study houses, markets, courtyards packed full with Jewish inhabitants. He can't properly conceive of Warsaw being *jüdenrein* or of Warsaw's Jewish streets as ruins. Many others are very likely experiencing the same thing. He also can't imagine the provincial towns of Poland without Jews. What does that even mean? How is it possible that a shtetl in Poland has no synagogue or study house? How can there be a Friday without the bathhouse being heated, without Jewish wives baking hallahs and preparing a pot of cholent? The imagination refuses to submit to logic. And another thing: this writer cannot imagine that all of his relatives, all of his friends, everyone he knows and holds dear and whom he left behind, lie dead, slaughtered and incinerated. In his imagination he is talking to all of them, doing business with them, arguing with them, and judging them according to their good and bad qualities. It's difficult to imagine that everything has been turned literally into ashes.

In a certain sense, this powerlessness of the imagination is our excuse. Future generations of Jews may wonder how, during these days and months, we could have eaten, drunk, done any sort of business, gone to the theater, and lived like always. The answer is that the tragedy was too great for our little minds.

Our eyes can't see extremely short ultraviolet rays. Our ears don't hear sounds that are too high-pitched.

We don't possess the senses needed to feel the greatest human sorrow multiplied by hundreds of thousands or millions. Years will pass before the Jewish people are able to account for the blow we have been struck and for the villainy of the German people.

The thing about Warsaw's streets was that each had its own character, its unique atmosphere. This is partly true of New York too. Fifth Avenue has a different character than does a street in the Bronx. East Broadway is different from 14th Street. But the streets in New York change their characters so quickly that as soon as you succeed in defining the atmosphere of one or another area there's already been a change. Here you're constantly having to move. Buildings are torn down. They change how to get from one place to another. New York is a city that's still being built. The situation in Warsaw was completely different, especially in the part where the majority of Jews lived. Everything was old, long established. If a street looked a certain way, that's how it stayed.

Warsaw Jews split Warsaw into "these streets" and "those streets." Obviously, wherever they lived was considered "*these* streets." Generally speaking, the split was between southern Warsaw and northern Warsaw, though had there been a subway in Warsaw you could have traveled from "these streets" to "those streets" in a matter of minutes. But there was no subway. In fact, there were Jews who had spent long years living on "these streets" and in that whole time had never been to "those streets." There was a kind of local patriotism among the inhabitants of both parts of Warsaw.

For us, what we called "these streets"—the southern part of the Jewish streets—included Śliska, Panska, Grzybowska, Twarda, Grzybowski Square, Gnojna, Krochmalna, Mariańska, and a few others. It's hard to say why, but the inhabitants of these particular streets considered themselves *real* Warsawians. Litvak Jews rarely stumbled their way here. On Shabbat, Hasidic Jews in this area would walk around in large fur hats. The most strictly religious and orthodox Warsaw Jews were concentrated in this part of the city. There were no big businesses here. There were mostly small shops that sold herbs, spices, milk, sweets, coal. Most of the Jews here were poor. But as soon as people here became wealthy, they were as solid as nobility, without debts, mortgages, or bankruptcies. Here, on "these streets," every courtyard had its own Hasidic prayer house and in every few courtyards, a ritual bath. The young men and boys who studied Torah here rarely tucked their sidelocks behind their ears. It wasn't necessary. You often saw old women here who were completely bent over, in large head coverings with colored satin ribbons hanging in the back. People with mental illness walked the streets freely, and children would chase after them them. The beggars each had their own areas staked out, their own territories. The largest handout here was a groschen, the smallest was a bit of sugar. As strange as it sounds, the Haskalah, modern secular life, arrived here very slowly and very late. At a time when "those streets" were teeming with Zionists, Bundists, populists, and other freethinkers, seculars were still a rare sight in this area. As soon as a young man here left religion, he was considered a thoroughly sinful Jew and sooner or later left "these streets."

"These streets" loved nothing more than rabbis and Hasidic rebbes. When a reputable rebbe came to Warsaw, he usually stayed on "these streets." Here he had all his conveniences. There were no trams in most of these streets. Hasidim could fill the streets undisturbed. True, when the rebbe needed money, it was time to go visit the wealthy people in "those streets." But the path that brought him to the next world was better followed from here.

Famous rabbis once lived on "these streets," including Rabbi Zanvil Klepfisz and Rabbi Itsikel, whose last name I've forgotten. There was a Hasidic prayer house at Krochmalna No. 5 where none other than Rabbi Itshe Alter, the author of *Hidushei HaRim* and grandfather of today's Gerrer Rebbe, once studied. The wars between the Ger and Aleksander Hasidim were waged on these streets. Here some of the minor Hasidic rebbes had their sworn followers: the Amshinover, the Sochatchover, the Radzyminer, the Minsker, the Nayshteter. On Friday evenings the Shabbat patrol would go around and make sure that everyone closed their shops early. A shop open on Shabbat was unheard of here. On Shabbat mornings, the streets in this part smelled like cholent and kugel. Shabbat songs rang out of every window. Here in "these streets" it was the Land of Israel.

It's worth noting that the underworld preferred "these streets" to "those streets." True, in "those streets" you could pull off a sizable heist, but lying low was better done in "these streets." Here the thieves had their own taverns, their own little restaurants and "hostels" where they stopped over. Here they also had their mistresses. Just as in the Hasidic houses everyone was extremely Hasidic, here in the indecent houses everyone was extremely indecent . . .

The "other streets" included Dzielna, Pawia, Gęsia, Miła, Niska, Stawki, Muranów, and above all Nalewki and Franciszkańska. There was constant chaos in this part. Before the war, Jews in this part did business with Vladivostok, Petropavlovsk, and with China. There were also very large businesses there, packed with merchandise to the ceiling. Rents were high here because every apartment contained its own business. There were countless small factories too. Here there was always the bustle of a neighborhood that's busy up to its neck with trade. There were study houses here too, but you couldn't see them for all of the businesses, factories, and workshops that surrounded them. People here did not walk but raced around, and when they wanted to go from one street to another they "caught a tram." From here, thousands of traveling salesmen went out to the farthest regions to sell merchandise. In the restaurants and local hotels (which were all known as Hôtel de Bedbug), they told jokes and stories about their exploits. When you told a funny story here, a "wily tale," no one asked you whether it was true or false. What was the difference? As long as it was a good one. When a merchant in this part said that he had just gotten back from Siberia (we're talking about the time of the Russian Empire), no one was surprised.

It was common on "those streets" that almost every apartment was also a business or else had furnished rooms for rent. People here were constantly doing business. On Gęsia there were enormous fabric dealers from which all of Poland bought their material. People talked about whether stocks were rising or falling. They were interested in foreign currency, whether the English pound sterling had gone up or down. Hasidic Jews wore stiff collars and neckties since it was "good for business." In this area, people dreamed about building up the Land of Israel and about social revolutions. This was where you picked up Yiddish newspapers in the morning, and this was the place into which hordes of Litvak Jews streamed.

When Warsaw Jews from "these streets" said "Litvak," they weren't only referring to Jews from Lithuania. A Litvak was anyone who, saying the Yiddish word for "I," said not "*yakh*" but "*ikh*." They could be Jews from Ukraine, Volyn, Podil, Russia—they were all considered Litvaks. The Jews who said "*yekh*" instead of either "*yakh*" or "*ikh*" were exceptions, and they were called "provincial," which is to say, from the provinces of Poland.

Jews from "these streets" could never understand the Litvaks. They were stingy and hungry for money. They never visited any rebbes and completely muddled up every Yiddish word. They wore short jackets, like the Germans, but at the same time they studied the Talmud in groups and at all kinds of Litvak schools. The serious Litvaks went to afternoon prayers early. There were synagogues in "those streets" where they were already saying afternoon prayers at one o'clock. On top of that, the Litvaks were experienced merchants, schemers. The Jews of "these streets" could not understand any of this. They looked at the Litvaks with the same sort of astonishment and revulsion with which Christians look at Jewish immigrants. Everything about them was somehow wild, unusual, dangerous.

Only in later years, when the youth from "these streets" started "going bad," did people start to get closer to those who lived on "those streets." There were times when a match between a Polish Jew and a Litvak was considered an unnatural and crazy thing.

Jewish life in general stood out for its lively character. People made merry at weddings and wailed at funerals. When something happened out on the street there was soon a free-for-all. When a Warsaw woman had a love affair, she burned like fire. When two men had a disagreement, they went straight to the rabbinical court. The religious folk would literally die for God. The unbelievers came to be called libertines. When a woman from Warsaw sang a hit song, she put a lot of heart into it. When a fishwife or goosemonger sang the praises of her goods, she'd say that there hasn't been a fish or a goose like hers since the beginning of the world and that a single whiff would bring you health. There was one thing that was totally foreign to Warsaw Jews, and this was *indifference*.

It isn't easy to imagine that this pulsating and animated way of life has been extinguished. It's inconceivable that this enormous collective of human uniqueness has been wiped out.

This article continues Singer's interest in Jewish customs and traditions, revisited in the years of the Holocaust, during which the need to pass them on to a younger generation became acute as the older one was being annihilated. This piece is included in the collection because it represents an exploration of the religious laws around a common yet problematic practice invoked by Singer in many novels and stories, and a recurring theme of animal cruelty: swinging chickens by the neck before being slaughtered to symbolize the kind of sacrifice that was made during the times of Temple Judaism.

Famous Rabbis Who Spoke Out against Swinging Chickens as a Sacrifice before Yom Kippur

(September 24, 1944)

The custom of *shlogn kapores*, swinging chickens as a sacrifice of atonement before Yom Kippur, is very old. But it's a custom, not a law. Moreover, there are many religious authorities who believe that it's a bad custom. The *Shulhan Arukh*, for example, states plain and simple that the custom of swinging chickens by the neck before Yom Kippur must be avoided. The *Shulhan Arukh* was authored by Rabbi Joseph Karo, who lived in the city of Safed in the Land of Israel. People who don't approve and don't want to swing chickens by the neck can point to his book as saying that it isn't a good custom.

How did Jews come to swinging chickens before Yom Kippur? How is it possible that religious Jews violate an injunction from the *Shulhan Arukh*?

The answer is that the *Shulhan Arukh* consists of two parts, the words of Rabbi Joseph Karo and commentaries written by Rabbi Moshe Isserles, or, as he is called, the Rama. Rabbi Karo was from the Land of Israel, but Rabbi Isserles was from Poland. He was Galician, the rabbi of Kraków. Rabbi Isserles's commentaries were as holy for Jews in Poland as Rabbi Karo's words. And Rabbi Isserles said that Jews *should* follow this custom. He said it was an accepted custom for men to swing a rooster by the neck and for women to do it with a hen.

If the woman is pregnant, she should swing a hen *and* a rooster, because if the child in her womb is a boy he can't fulfill the custom with a hen alone. It has to be a rooster. The Rama says that there's also a custom of looking for white chickens for the sacrificial ritual. The intestines of the slaughtered chickens should be thrown onto the roof so that they could be enjoyed by the birds.

So the fact that religious Jews everywhere still swing chickens as part of the sacrificial ritual shows that they side with the Rama's words more than they do with Rabbi Karo's. Why is this the case? Rabbi Karo was senior!

There are a few explanations for this. First, Rabbi Joseph Karo said no, and Rabbi Isserles said yes, and religious Jews have always preferred a yes to a no. When it comes to a mitzvah or a law that has to do with redemption from sin, Jews don't want to take any chances. Anyway, for both the meal ahead of Yom Kippur and the meal afterward, you're supposed to prepare meat. So why not swing a chicken at the same time? Why not try laying your sins onto a stupid hen or rooster?

Second, the kabbalists—those who gave themselves over to studying hidden teachings and the secrets of the Torah—believed that you *should* swing chickens as a sacrifice. The greatest Jewish kabbalist is considered to be Rabbi Isaac Luria, the Ari, who lived in the Land of Israel almost at the same time as Rabbi Karo. Rabbi Luria approved of the custom of swinging chickens. He even said that the best thing is to slaughter the chicken very early on the morning of Yom Kippur Eve, before dawn, after the penitential prayers, since this is a time of great mercy in the heavens, of great pity. Rabbi Isaiah Horowitz—another great and eminent kabbalist who wrote *Two Tablets of the Covenant* (also called the holy *Shelah*)—said the same thing. So Rabbi Isserles had the support of the kabbalists.

A third explanation is that when it comes to the Torah, there is always a bit of local patriotism.

Rabbi Isserles was a Polish rabbi, and the Polish Jews were quicker to side with him than with Rabbi Karo, who'd lived in faraway lands. Naturally, they also strictly followed Rabbi Karo, but when there was a disagreement about a law between the two, Polish Jews followed their fellow Polish-born rabbi. In that time, people didn't make the same distinction between today's Galicia, Poland, and Lithuania. Jews from Kraków, Lublin, or Vilnius were all Polish Jews, and for all of them Rabbi Isserles was a great and local authority. Since Polish Jewry had for hundreds of years produced the greatest Talmudic scholars, this held sway in the religious Jewish world, and Jews all over the world followed the example of the Polish Jews.

This begs the question: But why was there a conflict over swinging chickens in the first place? Why did one side believe that you *should* and the other that you should *not*? What were the reasons, the motivations?

The answer is that swinging chickens is in many senses an evocation of offering sacrifices. Long ago, in the time of the Temple, Jews would offer sacrifices. A sacrifice was offered every morning. There were special sacrifices made on Shabbat, on the first day of every month, and on each separate holiday. Aside from this, private people were also able to offer their own sacrifices. When Jews sinned and feared being punished by God, they brought a *korban hatat*, a sin offering. The sinning people laid their hands on the sacrifice and confessed their sins. The people were redeemed once the sacrifice took their sins upon itself.

The holiest sacrifice was made by the Kohen Gadol, the Great Priest, on Yom Kippur. This sacrifice redeemed the sins of all Jews. The ritual in which the Kohen Gadol went into the Holy of Holies was extremely important and evoked pious trembling among everyone. In the liturgy for Yom Kippur, there's a part called *Avoda*, and in this prayer there's an explanation of the many details involved in the Kohen Gadol's holy worship during Yom Kippur. During part of this prayer, we kneel or prostrate ourselves in memory of the old times when Jews knelt in the courtyard of the Temple.

So taking a rooster or a hen and swinging it evokes these sacrifices, though at the time they used neither hens nor roosters.

Those who believe we should not swing chickens explain that since the Temple has been destroyed and the Jews have been sent into exile, there's no sense in doing anything that evokes offering sacrifices. We are forbidden from offering sacrifices anywhere but in the Land of Israel in the Temple. Offering a sacrifice in the wrong place is itself a great sin. Either we offer a sacrifice according to all the laws or we don't offer one at all. Swinging chickens is a kind of compromise, a concession, and this is why many rabbis believed that it did more harm than good . . .

These were the arguments of those who were *against* the practice.

Those who *supported* swinging chickens expressed the sentiment of the people. This was a folk custom. Simple people like the idea of taking a living creature and transforming it into a sacrifice—a scapegoat. This ritual touched upon deep, ancient human emotions, half-forgotten instincts. Jews, just like people of other nations, like ritual—they like their religion to be concrete. Swinging chickens was ceremonial, it was expressive. Jews who had sinned all year long would pick up a chicken, swing it over their heads, and say, "This is my atonement, this is my offering, this stands in my place." In other words, anything I've done wrong will pass into its head and its body and its life . . .

Modern Jews very rarely partake in ceremonies. They have no Shabbat and no Jewish holidays. Their lives are gray, monotone. Modern Jewish leaders will need to think long and hard about how to bring some more liveliness and joy into Jewish life—a little more ceremony and festiveness.

Whereas earlier pieces in this collection explore the theme of good and evil through demonology and mysticism, this piece investigates the moral aspect of the issue, particularly in relation to human behavior and the psychological conditions of committing crimes or sins. Written four years after Singer began broaching the topic of evil in his articles at the outbreak of World War II, the piece aims to lay out a Jewish ethics that is specific to both the tradition and the psychology of the religious environment in which Singer grew up as well as the intellectual atmosphere of his young adulthood in interwar Poland.

The Ancient Jewish Notion that Good and Evil Are Always Battling Inside Us

(October 30, 1944)

Religious Jews believe that there are two angels: the Good Spirit and the Evil Spirit. The Good Spirit persuades us to do good. The Evil Spirit persuades us to do evil. But people have choice, a free will, in deciding between these two—the good and the evil. Human free will determines who is victorious, the Evil Spirit or the Good Spirit.

In the eyes of many thinkers, this conception appeared false and highly primitive. First, they did not believe in angels. Second, even if they accepted that the Good Spirit and the Evil Spirit were not angels but rather reflected the good and evil inclinations that exist *within* humankind, they still couldn't agree with this viewpoint. A long line of philosophers believed that people do *not* have free will. Just as there are reasons for why the heart beats quickly or slowly, why the stomach works better or worse, so there are reasons that determine why a person acts one way or another. For example, when we see people who are upset at others and insult them, we may think that it has something to do with their free will. They could have controlled themselves, but they didn't want to do so. But these philosophers did not believe this to be the case. If we knew the human body precisely, with all its glands and nerves, and also precisely how they all worked, we would see that this person had no choice.

Just as a machine has to move in the direction it's driven, people have to act as they act.

This question has led to great battles among philosophers. Those who *did* believe in free will argued that if people did not have free will, how could they ever be punished for crimes? They *had* to commit their crimes. So why did they deserve punishment? Those who *did not* believe in free will answered: they don't deserve it, but just as they had to commit their sin, so the judges and the police have to do their part.

This means that the world is an infinitely complicated machine where each screw has its own purpose. Everything is driven by predetermined forces. When people think that they're doing something out of free will, this is a fabrication. If a screw in a machine were capable of thinking, it might also believe that it's turning out of free will.

These discussions can go on forever. Logic won't help very much with this. Later philosophers recognized it as a problem that cannot be solved. Immanuel Kant made the following compromise: The question of whether or not there is free will indeed cannot be solved. But for human beings to be good, they have to accept that there is such a thing as free will. Since humankind has an impulse for goodness, or a conscience, people must also believe that there is a free will. In other words, practically speaking, we can't do without the idea of free will. Practical understanding dictates that humans are free.

All religions have, obviously, defended the idea of free will. How can people choose the way of God and reject the temptations of Satan if there is no free will?

Those who believe in historical materialism have denied the existence of free will. According to the teachings of Karl Marx and his followers, history leads us along a predetermined path, and we can't turn back the wheels of history or guide them in another direction. In this regard, historical materialism goes hand in hand with the materialists of former generations.

But even Marx believed that, practically speaking, we had to accept that humankind had free will. When Marx preached that the working class should unite and fight, he had to accept the necessity of agitation somewhere. No Marxists have ever reached the point where they left everything up to history. Practical life has shown us, at every step of the way, that if you take an action you may reach your goal, and if you take no action you reach nothing. No one can exist on philosophy alone.

It's interesting that modern psychologists, who call themselves psychoanalysts (analysts of the human soul), have completely gone back to the old-fashioned concept of the Good Spirit and the Evil Spirit. True, they don't use these very same words, but the meaning is the same: it's the same idea wearing a different veil. They believe that all of civilization is a product of self control. Humanity is, at its core, beastly, but a beast that can control itself. Plenty of times, when we're angry with someone, we want to punch them or even kill them. But we grit our teeth and stay quiet. Plenty of men would force themselves on women, curse and abuse others, throw stones, or do all kinds of other crazy things if they were not able to restrain themselves. A beast lies tied up in all of us. At certain times, the beast tears itself free from the rope and we commit a sin. There are times when entire masses of people throw off their self control. But one way or another they have to tie the beast back up. Human society cannot exist without self control. And with each generation, this self control gets more powerful. The more complicated life gets, the more we progress, the tighter we have to pull the rope around the neck of the beast that sits within us . . .

Sigmund Freud wrote a book called *Civilization and Its Discontents* where he showed the great price that humanity has paid for the self control that culture and civilization demand from us. We tie up the beast, but we suffer for it. In many cases, what suffers is our health.

This conception corresponds at least partially to the Jewish conception. The Hebrew Bible says that human nature is evil from early childhood. Jews never held the conviction that people were born good, as did the Chinese philosopher Confucius. No, humans were born as animals. But they were given the freedom to choose between good and evil, between life and death. The Godhead created a beast inside human beings, but it also gave us the power to rule it, to tame it. Within us, the Good Spirit and the Evil Spirit are constantly battling.

The Jewish religion placed a lot of emphasis on the idea that no matter how much people fight the evil inside them, they can never fully win. Even Moses sinned. The Jewish religion does not allow for the idea that anyone can be born holy, and certainly not that any human being can be God's child. Every person's goal is to *fight* against evil. So how can a person be born good from the start? How can we win the war before it has even started? . . .

But there's one fundamental difference between the religious conception of the Good Spirit and the Evil Spirit and the psychoanalytic conception. Religion believes that the less we listen to the beast, the better. People must not listen to all of the Evil Spirit's arguments. The Talmud says that if you run into this scoundrel (the Evil Spirit), drag him away to the study house. Jews believed that the best way was to ignore evil, not listen to it, not pay it any attention. The more we think about the wild instincts, the more power we give them. This is why the Jewish religion never thought highly of those who *fully* renounced the material world. A person who never married and who always lived alone had to think about improper things. It was better to indulge the instincts, but to a degree, in a respectable manner. The Jewish religion called for taming the beast, not for killing it . . .

The psychoanalysts believe that ignoring the instincts can often be dangerous. Their solution is to *get to know* your Evil Spirit! Get to know all of its ways and methods!

Almost all of modern culture, especially art, constitutes a study of the Evil Spirit. People of the modern period are great experts on the Evil Spirit. They are knowledgeable about every sort of passion, every evil inclination, every trap that the Evil Spirit sets for them. But does this leave them any better off? . . .

Religious Jews believe that the best thing for the soul is to be lazy, not to know too much about worldly matters. They believe that when we get to know the beast inside too well, when we are able to identify its every muscle and nerve, we start to acquire a love for it, and then instead of taming it we loosen all its bonds and set it free.

The Jewish religion teaches: Don't think too much about your enemy. Try not to engage deeply with its arguments. If you've come to a decision that it's your adversary, keep it bound up and shut its mouth . . . Why analyze the Devil when you can ignore him? The entirety of Jewish ethics is built on this viewpoint.

With the tide of World War II turning in the direction of the Allies, Singer seems to shift gears, beginning to take stock of where Yiddish language, culture, and literature will all find themselves once it ends—and where, in turn, this will leave him as a writer. He returns to a theme that seems to characterize, for him, the Jewish response to this historical moment—indifference to the fate of Yiddish and Yiddishkayt—but expresses a measure of what might be called pessimistic faith in its resilience and endurance. He argues for a path forward that is focused on a commitment to Yiddish that neither overdramatizes the crisis nor ignores its severity. He instead advocates for a third approach: acknowledging the existing difficulties while thinking creatively about how to address them given the historical reality that will exist in the postwar era. This approach reveals Singer both as a pragmatist and an adherent of Yiddish language and culture.

Yiddish Language and Culture Undergo Their Greatest Crisis in History

(December 4, 1944)

You don't have to be a sworn pessimist to maintain that Yiddish language and culture are going through their greatest crisis in history. Even the sworn optimists have admitted this. While it can be discussed at length, we will make an effort to offer in brief some of the causes.

The first and foremost reason is the tragedy of the Polish Jewish population. Poland was the home of Yiddish. In Poland, not only old people spoke Yiddish but children did too. It was a living language, though it led a life of poverty. The destruction of the Jews in Poland, Galicia, Lithuania, and Ukraine has simultaneously brought with it the destruction of Yiddish.

Naturally, today, there is no point in lamenting the destruction of the language. Living humans are more important than anything else. But we are merely confirming the fact here that with the destruction of East European Jewry, the sources of the Yiddish language have also been wiped away. This is a loss that will never be regained. Even if a few Jews live in these places after the war, there is no hope of a Yiddish revival there. The number of Jews is too small. The children who are still alive have lived with Christian families. Naturally, the surviving Jews will speak Yiddish, but there can be no more talk of an extensive Jewish population. Traditions have been ripped up. Communities that have existed for hundreds of years have been wiped out. Yiddishkayt has been pulled up by the roots. Yiddish writers in America can no longer hold the belief that they're writing for Jews from the other side of the ocean. Yiddish theater can no longer rely on those Jews. The former Polish Republic will most likely be split into two, between Russia and a new Poland, and there will be all kinds of political complications.

The second most important reason is that in the countries where many Jews living today still speak Yiddish and read Yiddish newspapers—like the United States, Argentina, Canada—the young people speak no Yiddish. You can point to this or that exception. There are Yiddish schools where kids learn Yiddish after they come back from middle school or high school. But a few swallows don't make a summer. It's a fact that the Yiddish press is losing readers. When Yiddish readers die, there's no one to take their place. The situation is such that the great majority of Jews who read Yiddish are old, and they will not live forever.

Just ten or fifteen years ago such claims were considered pessimistic and bleak. The optimists said that Jews were not subject to everyday laws. Something will happen! There'll be a miracle! The number of such optimists is quite small today. The facts are hitting us in the face. Today you hear the same claims from ardent Yiddishists, educational leaders, teachers, and writers. The harsh numbers tell us the harsh truth.

This writer does not believe that Yiddish is dying—or that we should say Kaddish for the Yiddish language and for Yiddish culture. But there can be no doubt that Yiddish is living through a difficult and bitter crisis and that it's heading downhill. Patting our bellies while crying out that everything is fine today not only smacks of foolishness but also of indifference to Yiddish.

The friends of Yiddish are today split into two camps.

One camp believes that things really are bad but that there's no point in talking about it. They say, "Why tell sick people, over and over, that they're in a bad situation?" Or maybe they just think this to themselves. They believe that we should do what we can and leave the rest up to fate, or to history. Most of the Yiddishists belong to this camp.

The other camp, which includes fewer people, consists of protesters. They cry, "This is horrible! Yiddish is dying!" Others tease the optimists and say, "We foresaw this long ago." And others still have simply fallen into despair. Their world, their Yiddish culture, is disappearing on them, and they feel helpless, impotent, afraid. They hide in their personal corners. They simply can't look each other in the eye.

This writer believes that neither side is right in its approach.

Pretending not to know, putting on a brave face when things are so bad, is essentially a sign of great resignation. Keeping silent about a situation is the same thing as renouncing all hope. You only go silent when there's nothing left to talk about. Things are certainly not that bad for Yiddish yet.

Those who do cry out are mostly passive people.

They're satisfied with offering themselves and others bitter words. They develop a sort of penchant for self torture. For them, the difficult situation in which Yiddish finds itself is just an excuse not to do anything, even the little bit that's in their power. They arouse resentment among the first camp, which does what it can and keeps quiet about the rest.

This writer believes that today we need a third camp: true devotees of Yiddish who neither create illusions for themselves nor go off on pointless diatribes.

For almost two thousand years, Hebrew has been a "dead" language. Until a few decades ago, there was no hope of Hebrew ever being revived. But the "Holy Tongue" had its devotees. They were people who loved the Hebrew word. They devoted themselves with great rigor to Hebrew grammar. They wrote letters to their friends in Hebrew. They wrote Hebrew poetry. True, Hebrew has always been a holy language for Jews, the language of the Bible and the Talmud. Yiddish cannot ever hold as high a place in the hearts of learned Jews as the role that Hebrew once played for them. But we believe that Yiddish has absorbed into itself enough Jewish zest, enough Jewish charm, enough creative power for it to have *its own devotees*. Yiddish unquestionably has qualities that Hebrew does not have. It's a language that has served us faithfully for over five hundred years and that has engraved itself deep into our souls. Whether Yiddish rises or falls, there should still be Jews who are devoted to Yiddish and who are ready to serve the language in the same way that the Hebraists once served Hebrew—and still do today.

Yiddish literature has to be collected. We have to separate the wheat from the chaff. We have to create the great, comprehensive Yiddish dictionary, we have to collect all of the linguistic and cultural treasures connected to Yiddish. This has to be done regardless of Yiddish either dying or staying alive.

We Jews have never, in our history, chased after rising stars and successes. We loved Hebrew, though for others it was "dead." We never completely forgot the Aramaic language that Jews once used to speak and write, though many hundreds of years have passed and we no longer use Aramaic in our everyday conversations. Why should Yiddish be an exception? Why should we demand that Yiddish be an unconditional success? Why should we check Yiddish's pulse every day to see how it's doing?

We spoke earlier of two camps among the Yiddishists. The first camp commits the error of not admitting that Yiddish is sick and is in need of special care and love. They got it into their heads at some point that Yiddish will stay the language of the Jewish masses, and they're afraid to think of a time when this situation will come to an end. Yiddish and the Jewish masses are so closely linked for them that they can't imagine one without the other.

The facts show that there is an error in this understanding. There's a good chance that Yiddish will, in the future, *not* be the language of the masses.

The second camp has realized that the Jewish masses will not speak Yiddish in the future, but because of this they want to make a complete break with Yiddish. Their logic is: either success or death.

Both camps, ultimately, have the same approach: if Yiddish can't develop, cannot be as vital as, say, English or French, it is washed up.

This is false and goes against all of our experience throughout our long history. We have never made our love dependent on "success."

Here Singer takes the holiday of Hanukkah as an opportunity to show how historical Jewish consciousness can be bound to contemporary crises—and at the same time demonstrates how he turns them into literary scenes with living characters, settings, and conflicts. We see too the seeds for *The Slave*, a novel he would write over a decade later, which appeared serially in Yiddish in 1961 but projected these same sensations into the past, setting the book in the 17th century. It is also a testament to Singer's faith in survivors—characters about whom he went on to write for decades. We see that his focus on Holocaust survivors was neither incidental nor exploitative after the fact. He was reflecting on their fates, imagining their stories, before he even met them—before they even knew they would survive World War II.

Hanukkah Candles and the Stories They Tell

(December 12, 1944)

There are moments in everyone's lives when they wish
they were old. They think that by the time they're old
they will have saved their nest egg, settled their children,
have the chance to retire from their business or job, and
live a life of rest for a while. But experience shows that
old age is rarely a time of rest. Old age brings forth new
problems, new struggles, new worries. According to the
Talmud, there's no rest even after death. The evildoers
are punished in Gehenna, and the righteous go from one
Garden of Eden to another, from one heavenly place to
the next. In short, there's no such thing as rest.

The same can certainly be said about the life of a
nation. Every nation hopes that after winning this or that
war, true rest will come, a long-coveted respite. But instead new battles immediately appear, new revolutions,
new enemies. Each time we have to start over again.

Jews have had less rest than any other nation in the
world. It's likely that we too once hoped that later, in the
far future, in old age, we might have a little rest. But the
older we get the bigger our troubles—and dangers. Our
problems grow so quickly that our every step, our every
breath, presents us with problems. You sometimes get
the sense that this will last forever. Another two thousand
years will pass, or another four thousand years, and the
Jews of the future will ask: How will we get ourselves out

of all these messes? How will we extricate ourselves from these countless dangers that lie in wait for us?

But beneath these dark thoughts, which befall every Jewish person who really cares about our fate, there's a deeper faith that our thorny path is not meaningless. That despite all of the difficulties and suffering we nevertheless move ahead, if not in a material sense then in a spiritual one.

The following words appear in the prayer that we say on Hanukkah: "In the days of Mattathias son of Yohanan the high priest, the Hasmonean, and his sons, the evil kingdom of Greece stood against your people Israel in order to make them forget your Torah and violate your laws. But You, in Your great mercy, stood up for them in their time of need, upheld their cause, judged their case, and avenged them. You delivered the mighty into the hands of the weak, the many into the hands of the few, the impure into the hands of the pure, the wicked into the hands of the righteous," and so on.

This faith, that sooner or later the just and not the powerful will be victorious, the righteous and not the wicked, sustained the Jewish people in its darkest times. This faith is deeply rooted in us today as well. The miracle of the Hasmoneans, the few Jewish heroes who withstood the numerous and powerful Greeks, is not a singular case in our history but rather expresses our national worldview, our perspective on life and humanity. Without this very faith, we couldn't have existed even a single day . . .

We Jews have staked everything on this faith. Jews who strive for Zionism or socialism or both pin all their hopes on the belief that the strongest will not have the last word in the history of the world.

This is why Hanukkah, in a broader sense, is not only a holiday for strictly religious Jews. We all light Hanukkah candles in some symbolic manner. Every one of us hopes that these tiny little candles—which the slightest wind can blow out and which give off more smoke than light—will one day all transform into a great light that will illuminate all nations and all peoples.

If there are still any Jews left under Hitler's rule, hiding in cellars, in ruins, in forests, they surely remember that today is Hanukkah. And who knows? Maybe they're secretly lighting a candle.

We try to imagine the following picture: Somewhere, in a Polish village still occupied by the Nazis, a Jewish man is hiding. He wears peasant garb, speaks Polish with the peasants, he goes to church and does everything possible to fit in. He knows that the slightest suspicion could cost him his life and the lives of those sheltering him. But this very same "peasant" has hidden a Jewish calendar somewhere in a barn, and he knows that today is the twenty-fifth day of Kislev. The day is short. Nighttime comes early. The peasant for whom he works as a farmhand goes to sleep early. The man goes into the barn, bolts the door behind him, and with a trembling hand takes out a piece of a candle. He lights it and sets it out on a board. He recites the blessing for lighting the Hanukkah candles and a special *Shehehiyanu* blessing to thank God for living to see this day. And who knows? Maybe he's hidden a small prayer book among the straw and is reciting the words to "Maoz Tzur," the song that

Jews sing by the light of Hanukkah candles . . .

He's an interesting Jew. He has no beard. He wears a sheepskin cap, a tattered fur coat, and rags wrapped around his feet. His face is sunburned, withered, sunken. On his upper lip he's grown a mustache, which he twists up on either side to look more like a peasant. But this "peasant" has a pair of sad Jewish eyes and a high Jewish brow. The soft glow of the Hanukkah candle dances in these eyes, and they exude not only sadness but also joy. What a stunt—lighting Hanukkah candles right under Hitler's nose! How many countless dangers has this man overcome in order to reach this very point! . . .

This man is not a product of this writer's imagination. He exists. There are many like him, both religious and secular, Jews with all sorts of hopes and ideals. He is one of the weak and pure who will survive the powerful and impure. He himself represents the miracle of Hanukkah in our time.

This article provides another example of the deliberateness of Singer's literary vision, in this case when it comes to choosing names for his characters. Each name has associations concerning both its cultural function and also its origins—which includes a mix of Greek, Latin, French, Italian, Polish—each being connected to some Hebrew name not used in daily life. Singer later adapted some of the choices made in Yiddish when translating the English versions of his stories, so while the Yiddish original of "The Destruction of Kreshev" featured a father named Reb Gimpl, the father in the English translation was Reb Bunem—a name that carried different associations and more thematically got across the idea of the father being a *bon-homme* in French, an *ish tov* in Hebrew, or "a good person" in English. The name Grunem, which also makes a cameo in this article and is placed in a comedic context, was later featured as a central character in Singer's stories about the fools of Chelm. The text of the article suggests that Singer bases it partly on a book about Jewish and Yiddish names published in Palestine around the time of his writing.

Jewish Names and Yiddish Names

(February 4, February 11, and March 4, 1944)

The history of the Jewish nation, especially its wandering, plays itself out in Jewish names. If no other document from Jewish history remained, there would still be a lot to learn from them.

The first sort of Jewish names consists of those mentioned in the Hebrew Bible: Abraham, Isaac, Jacob, the names of the tribes and so on. It's interesting that even in the Bible there are Jewish names that are not Hebrew but from other languages. When Joseph ended up in Egypt, he was given an Egyptian name, Zaphnath-Paaneah. The name Pinhas (Phineas) is Egyptian, and, at least according to Bible critics, it means "a black person." The name Mordechai is not Hebrew but Babylonian. It seems that the same is true of Esther. The name Job is not Hebrew but rather Edomite, from the land of Edom, which was near Palestine and where, according to the Bible, Esau's grandchildren lived. The Bible critics also maintain that the name Ruth is not Hebrew but rather came from the Hittite people, against whom Jews fought a war when they took the Land of Israel.

Bible critics go even further. They maintain that Moshe (Moses) isn't a Hebrew name but rather Egyptian, though no Egyptian documents have ever been found with the name Moshe . . .

Many of the Jewish names mentioned in the Hebrew Bible have a meaning. The name Yitskhak (Isaac) means "He will laugh." . . . At that time, people hadn't yet started naming babies after grandfathers or grandmothers but rather based them on events or feelings that were connected with the birth . . . After leaving Palestine—and even for a time before, while Palestine was ruled by the Greeks and the Romans—many Jews gave their children Greek and Roman names. Some of these names have remained to this day. The name Alexander is not Hebrew. It's the name of the Greek emperor Alexander the Great. A great many Jewish high priests, kings, and political leaders have had Greek and Roman names, including Talmi (Ptolemy), Yanai (Jannaeus), and Hordus (Herod). Many Talmudic scholars bore Babylonian names. Already in these ancient times there were Jews who had two names, one Jewish and one from the local kingdom where they lived . . .

A work was recently published in Palestine in ten volumes in which all Jewish names are said to be found, but it's difficult to believe that all of the names that Jews have ever been given in all of their history could fit into ten volumes . . .

Many Yiddish names come from German. Blume, Freyde, Royze, Gele, Grine, Sheyne, Feyge, Ziskind, Zisl, Alter, Alte, Gimpl, and many others sound German. Freyde is from *Freude*, which means "joy." Feyge is from *Vogel*, which means "bird." Ziskind is a *zis Kind*, a "sweet child." The name Brayne comes from *braun*, or "brown." Frume is the same as *fromm*, "religious." Gitl is the same as *Güte*, "goodness."

The name Tsharne is completely Polish. It means

"black." But it's interesting that there are no Christian Polish women named Tsharne. The word is indeed Polish, but the idea, so to speak, is Jewish. It's the same with many other Jewish names that sound German. When it came to giving names, Jewish parents had their own notions. They borrowed the words from the local language but not the ideas. In any case, these names are proof that our forebears once lived in Germany. They are documents of Jewish wandering.

Many Yiddish names actually come from Italian. The name Beyle sounds typically Yiddish to us. When you say that a woman is named Beyle, you imagine a woman in an apron or a head covering. But the name comes from *bella*, which means "beautiful" in Italian.

Believe it or not, the old-fashioned name Shprintse comes from Italian too. It's taken from the Italian word *speranza*, which means "hope." The Jewish name Bendit is actually Benedetto (Benedict), which means "to bless" and which is the same as the Hebrew name Baruch.

When you're told that a Jewish man is named Fayvish, you imagine a respectable homeowner, a man with a big beard, with a wide *tallis-kotn* beneath his shirt and a big tallis bag under his arm. And yet, believe it or not, Fayvish is named after the Greek god Phoebus, the god of light. This word is also the source of the name Fayvl. It's interesting that when a Jewish man named Fayvish or Fayvl is called to the Torah, he is called Shraga instead. In Aramaic, Shraga means "light." Those who linked the name Fayvish to Shraga knew where the name originated.

I read somewhere that the name Grunem is also from Italian. Grunem is a name we use in comedies to portray an old-fashioned man, a loafer, a fanatic. When you hear the name Grunem in the Yiddish theater you immediately start laughing. You know in advance that Reb Grunem will be a comic figure. Well, Grunem is an Italian name too. The first people who named their children Grunem did it because they wanted to be stylish, to go along with the times, to fit in with their surroundings. But with time, Jews left Italy, and the name Grunem became a deeply rooted Jewish name, the kind that only religious parents gave their children—parents who didn't take their surroundings into account but who held steadfastly onto tradition.

The name Yenta comes from the Italian word *gentile*, which means "a noble-born," an aristocrat. The first man who called his daughter Gentile (which later became Yentale and Yenta) could not have imagined that Yenta would one day become a name that represents everything old-fashioned, and that when someone says about a woman that she isn't very bright, but that she lives like her grandmother and great-grandmother, they'll call her a Yenta.

The name Bunem comes from the French word *bonhomme*, which refers to a good-natured and happy-go-lucky man who has very little wisdom. Bunem is called to the Torah as Simha-Bunem. The name Shneur comes from the French word *seigneur*, a nobleman. The old-fashioned name Toltse comes from the Italian *dolce*, which means "sweet."

If the Jewish exile lasts another two thousand years, it's possible that a religious Jewish woman with a head covering will be called Elizabeth, or Marion, and that a

Jewish man with a large tallit and tefillin will be called Lester, Mortimer, Herbert, or George . . .

Luckily we haven't only taken but also given. And we've taken more from ourselves than from others . . . There's a whole series of Jewish names that come in pairs. When a man named Leyb is called up to the Torah, people use the name Yehuda-Arye. Well, Arye is the Hebrew word for lion. But what is the name Yehuda doing here? The answer is that when Jacob blessed his children, he compared Yehuda to a young lion. This comparison linked the name Yehuda to Arye and then to Leyb. Jacob compared his son Binyamin to a wolf, and so you very often find the name Binyamin with the name Zev, which means "wolf" in Hebrew . . .

It's interesting that Jews have rarely used the many hundreds of names in the Hebrew Bible. Jews have used 2 or 3 percent at best . . . And it seems that these names will, at this point, never populate themselves among Jews. But the new Jewish population in the Land of Israel has latched on to them as to a buried treasure. The Hebraists don't want to give their daughters names like Perl, Brayne, Beyle, Blume, Yakhne, Hinde, Feyge, Libe, or their sons names like Hershl, Velvl, Zaynvl, Berl, Gimpl, Kopl, Fayvl. These names recall the exile. And so they've taken back the long-forgotten names found in the Hebrew Bible . . .

A name used by both men and women today is Zisl. You may encounter a woman named Zisl and a man named Zisl . . . But where does a name like Traytl come from? This writer has seen a religious book in which the name Traytl is linked with Yehuda. That was all he could find in the book . . . The rabbis who wrote books about names were quite uninterested in the history of a name or its meaning. They were mainly interested in the law governing how to spell the name in a divorce contract. This writer has found an entry in an old German dictionary of names that is similar to Traytl. The name is Trutelin . . .

Jews in Greater Poland and in the Polish shtetls along the Vistula have certainly heard of the name Eber. This writer himself knew a man by this name. It's an old German name. Jews certainly turned Abraham into the nickname Eber, or they gave their child two names, one that was Hebrew and one that was German. Another German name is Gets or Getsl. The name Zalman is usually linked to the name Shlomo. But there is also a German name, Salomon. The name Golda does not appear among old German names and is most likely a name that only Jews gave to their daughters . . .

In Poland and Russia you can find many Jews with Slavic-sounding names. Many Jews in Poland named themselves after the noblemen with whom they had dealings or after those cities where they lived. It's a shame that there is still no comprehensive and in-depth book written in Yiddish about Jewish names. It would elicit great interest among Yiddish readers.

It has always been customary for Jews to have "everyday" names and also corresponding "holy" names. These "everyday" names were names that did not sound Hebrew but rather German, Polish, Russian, or any other language. For example, a man who was called Itche, Itzik, Isaak, or Isidore had the "religious" name Yitskhak.

When he was called up to the Torah, people used his religious name, his "holy" name . . .

If a man is called by the name Gottlieb, his Hebrew name is most often Yedidya. Gottlieb is a translation of Yedidya, which literally means "God's friend." A man named Gutman or Gutkind is, in reality, Tevya . . . The name Gimpl is connected to Ephraim or to Mordechai . . .

Many readers will ask: Why is it that one name or another is connected to a particular everyday name? For example, what connects Menahem to Mendl?

The name Mendl was very likely a popular German name in the past. A man who had a son wanted him to have a secular name, a name of which he didn't have to be ashamed among Christians and which they could easy pronounce. But since Jews also had to have a Hebrew name, a name with which they were called up to the Torah, people connected names according to how they sounded, according to their first letter, according to the similarity of their meaning, or according to any other similarities. Mendel and Menahem are similar in that they both start with the letters "M-e-n" . . .

Every male "everyday" name was connected with a particular Hebrew name. But this was only true for men. Women were not called up to the Torah. So women did not need to have both an "everyday" name and a "holy" name . . .

Among the male names we noted some interesting ones, including Vaybl, which means "little wife." We can't say why a father would name his son Vaybl. Imagine a couple where the husband is named Vaybl, or "little wife," and the wife is named Leviya, or "lioness." It's an easy picture to paint: the pants are likely worn by the "lioness" and not by the "little wife."

Yiddish fiction writers have, till now, barely exploited these magnificent old Yiddish names.

With World War II over in Europe, Singer again shifts focus from a lament over a culture being lost to an artistic program that would invoke that culture in literary fiction for future generations. He had actually begun this shift with the essay mentioned earlier, "Problems of Yiddish Prose in America" (1943), and a second essay, "Concerning Yiddish Literature in Poland" (1943), which together laid out his critique of how Yiddish writers of his time conceived of their literary task going forward. In the latter essay he returned to the idea explored in the first—the need to go back to religious sources for inspiration going forward—this time framing it as a continuation of a literary approach set out by Y. L. Peretz: "the work begun by Peretz was groundbreaking. It revealed the beginning of the path that Yiddish literature would need to take if it was to exist at all." This statement gives context to his vitriol in the present article. He was himself an adherent of Peretz's path, but for him Peretz was a guidepost on the path, not a shrine at its end. Singer believed not in invoking Peretz's greatness for his own gain but in learning from his choices and, like him, going back to the religious sources of Jewish learning, wisdom, and culture to forge a path forward.

Was Y. L. Peretz a Writer or a Rebbe?

(July 9, 1945)

They say that the biblical Jacob asked for his bones to be brought to the Land of Israel because he feared that, after he died, the Egyptians would turn him into a god, an idol to worship. There's a great understanding of human nature in this explanation and even some humor. Since ancient times people have tended to turn great and prominent people into gods.

When great people first appear, people initially refuse to acknowledge them. They begrudge them the fact that they are greater than others, they look for all kinds of wrongdoings, they start fighting with them. As soon as they achieve their greatness, the same people, or their children, appear and want to turn them into gods or idols. They turn them into saints. They cry out that we all have to follow in their footsteps and that in no way can we, God forbid, stray right or left from their words. They forcefully turn them into leaders.

Little people don't do this out of admiration for great people. The majority of people are not generally capable of actual admiration. They do it because they want to warm themselves by someone else's fire, to be great on account of someone else. If a rebbe, a Hasidic leader, is a *great* rebbe, then automatically his Hasid, his follower, is great too, and anyone who utters a single word against his rebbe should watch out. The Hasid would really get fired up. He'd scream like someone possessed. He'd tear you apart limb from limb.

This is the kind of commotion that people are now making on the Yiddish literary scene about Y. L. Peretz.

The idea that Peretz was a great Yiddish writer is not enough for the literary "hasidim." They want to turn him unconditionally into a Hasidic rabbi, a rebbe. With the same fervor of old-time Hasidim who used to recount the marvels and tales of the Amshinover, Piazetsner, or Kozhnitser rebbes, so a long list of writers has now begun agitating to sanctify Peretz. These are the same little "hasidim" of the olden days but without beards, side-locks, or true faith.

Another thing: the old-time Hasidim spent a lot of money on their rebbes. The would-be "hasidim" in question want others to pay them for their contrived hasidism. If Peretz was a great writer, and I, Zekl son of Flekl, think highly of him, then this must mean that I'm great too—so you should throw me a party and read my poems. If not, it means you're an unbeliever.

This is, more or less, the logic of those who want to exploit Peretz's greatness for their own smallness.

The idea of turning a writer, a literary person, into a saint, a leader, a prophet is senseless from start to finish. It never occurred to any French person to turn Maupassant, Emile Zola, Victor Hugo, Flaubert, or any of the other great French authors into leaders. No Russian person with any common sense would call for following the ways of Pushkin, Lermontov, Dostoevsky, Chekhov, and all of the other Russian masters. Tolstoy did have a few followers, the Tolstoyans, but first, Tolstoy preached a religion, and second, most of the Tolstoyans were not great sages. Tolstoy himself considered them nuisances. You don't hear that Americans are trying to turn Edgar Allan Poe, Longfellow, Melville, Mark Twain, or any other writers into spiritual leaders. The English study Shakespeare's work, but Shakespeare is considered a playwright, not a person whose words have to be followed . . .

A new Hasidim has been created on the Jewish street. For a small number of Yiddishists, Peretz has become what Rabbi Nahman of Bratslav is for the Uman Hasidim: the rebbe who, though he is dead, lives forever. A number of cultural figures who are against the Land of Israel are trying to prove with all possible evidence that Peretz was a diasporist, that he believed in exile. Actually, it doesn't even matter if the rebbe believed in exile. We, his "hasidim," have to remain in exile and let ourselves be slaughtered. We wouldn't want to go and do anything different than what Peretz instructed us.

And others, who are Zionists, try to justify their Zionism unconditionally though Peretz. Luckily, Peretz was a person of varying moods. He spoke now like a Zionist, now like a Bundist, and later like a territorialist, so people can find in him whatever they seek . . .

The truth is that this whole "hasidism" that has grown around Peretz is built on the idea that *nothing* should be done, that there's no obligation to do anything. We don't even have to give this rebbe the customary gift.

Peretz was a great writer, and like every great writer he had his great qualities and his great flaws. The Peretzians are people who want to do nothing but babble. Peretz-Hasidism is built entirely on the idea that everything should stay the same.

To be an Amshinover Hasid you had to pray, study, send your children to heder, eat kosher food, let your beard and sidelocks grow, and accept a thousand burdens. To follow in "Peretz's path" you don't have to do anything except go to the Yiddish theater once a year or buy a chapbook from a poet. You're not even obligated to teach your children Yiddish. A great number of Peretzians haven't even sent their own children to Yiddish school. And anyway, why lie? Peretz himself didn't do this either.

This is a cheap Hasidism. Peretz would have totally rejected such rebbefication.

Written about two months after the Nazi surrender, this article shows Singer continuing his shift from the urgency of recollecting the past to finding a path toward portraying that past in literary fiction. It appeared just four months before he started serially publishing *The Family Moskat*, his first and most elaborate ode to Warsaw Jewry, further revealing the deliberateness of his undertaking. As in other similar articles, Singer continues placing Yiddish and Hebrew literature in related categories, yet his focus on Yiddish puts additional emphasis on the locale in which it grew and developed: the shtetl. In all, Singer puts forth a paradox, both critiquing Yiddish literature's focus on the shtetl and noting that it has no choice but to portray the shtetl from which it came. The resolution to this paradox is to look deeper into the spiritual riches that propped up the shtetl, not only its material poverty—to portray not its appearance from the outside but the internal fire that kept it alive for centuries.

Jews and Jewish Life Not Yet Portrayed in Yiddish Literature

(July 15, 1945)

Like the Jewish people, Yiddish literature is an interesting and complex phenomenon. It has certain features that make it different from all other literatures. What makes it different? The fact that it is very, very poor when compared with Jewish life. No other people has as great a chasm between its literature and its life as do the Jews.

Our life is immensely rich in events. Jews live in every part of the world, in every country. One Jew by the name of Cohen is a judge in Manhattan and another Cohen is a general in China. One Levi is a deputy, say, in the Argentinian parliament, another Levi is a psychiatrist in Paris, a third owns a diamond mine in South Africa, a fourth is a commissar in Moscow, and a fifth actually lives somewhere among the tribes of India. A sixth has a harem in Cairo. Jews speak every language in the world, are represented in almost every profession, play a role in every movement. From a literary perspective, the "international Jews" whom the fascists hate so much are actually treasures. They represent material for millions of literary topics. You meet Jews on every ship, every train. They take part in the majority of revolutions, they sit in every prison, they're connected with all kinds of industrial undertakings, they play all the stock markets, they study in every university that will have them, they're even found in the Vatican. Where aren't there Jews crowding together?! What kind of trouble don't they get into? Their reality is so fantastic that it can't be grasped even by the richest imaginations.

But when you start reading Yiddish literature, you get a whole different idea about Jews. It's as if Jews only did one thing: live in tiny shtetls and keep half-empty shops, scratching themselves or chewing straw out of immense boredom. If a Martian tried learning about the character of Jews from Yiddish literature, it would get the impression that no other people is as stuck in the mud, as backward, as provincial, as boring as Jews. It would not learn more from Hebrew literature. If the same Martian were able to leaf through the Jewish encyclopedias in Russian or English and see how many world-class scholars, politicians, millionaires, revolutionaries, prominent doctors, famous lawyers, inventors, opportunists who converted, actors, musicians, painters, university professors, editors, statesmen, military people, bankers, entrepreneurs, and other colorful personalities we had, it would cry in astonishment: *Why has Yiddish literature silenced them? Why do Yiddish writers omit all of these interesting personalities and characters? How can such a richness in life lead to the development of such a sparse and gray literature?*

The answer is that Yiddish literature developed in the small and gloomy shtetls in Poland and Lithuania, not in the big cities of the world. Yiddish writers, for the most part, know no more than one language, their little Yiddish. They either stay in the little shtetl where they were born or they make their way to New York or Buenos Aires, where they build themselves a spiritual ghetto.

To portray the Jewish professors, bankers, inventors, or millionaires, you have to know such people well, speak their language, know their business thoroughly. But Yiddish writers have no access to such environments. You can't portray what you don't know. A Yiddish literature that is attuned to the greatness of Jewish life in the full sense of the word has never existed.

We will go even further and say that such a literature can never exist. Writers can best depict people who speak the language in which they write. Dostoevsky's characters all speak Russian or a bit of French, which people spoke in Russia. Maupassant's characters speak French, while Dickens's characters speak English. The characters of all the great writers have all, for the most part, lived in the same country as the writers, spoke their language, shared the same customs, expressions, and traditions. This is why the writers knew them. They were their neighbors, their relatives.

But how can writers who speak Yiddish depict a Jew who speaks, let's say, French, and acts like a Frenchman? How can they portray a man with a harem in Egypt when he only speaks Arabic? For Yiddish writers to utilize all these Jewish themes they'd need to know thousands of languages and to have lived a long time in each country. They would have to have lived forever, have been a kind of Ahasver, an eternal wanderer who is familiar with everything, knows everything, and has experienced everything. Jews, as a group, do indeed have all of these merits, or demerits. But each individual Jew is limited by time and space.

Yiddish literature can only depict Yiddish-speaking

Jews and no others. So Yiddish literature is just an infinitely small part of literature about Jews—the literature that would need to reflect the great adventure that is itself the Jewish exile.

There are books in every language that have Jewish characters. Yet these books don't belong to one literature but to different literatures. Many such books were written not by our friends but by our enemies, or people indifferent to us. Jewish authors writing in different languages don't go chasing after Jewish topics. First, they don't always want to emphasize their Jewishness. And second, they know that a book with Jewish themes has a lesser chance of being read by large audiences than a book with general themes. The result is that we are a big people with a small literature. Our rich, adventurous life is silenced . . .

So despite the fact that Yiddish and Hebrew literature are little more than an insignificant part of what *should* be Jewish literature, together they actually constitute the *backbone* of Jewish literature. Their power lies not in how widely they're read, but in their *conception* . . . Only in Yiddish or in Hebrew are there fiction writers with a solid knowledge of Judaism. There are great Yiddish scholars writing academic works about Jews in English, in German, or in other languages. But we don't know a single fiction writer who has written about Jewish life in another language and possessed the kind of knowledge of Jewish life and culture that was held by Mendele Moykher Sforim, Sholem Aleichem, Y. L. Peretz, Haim Nahman Bialik, or S. Y. Agnon. This is why Yiddish and Hebrew writers have the right to be recognized as the true creators of Jewish literature.

This leads to the thought that Yiddish writers have to choose especially those topics and themes that reflect the Jewish spirit. We have less room for random themes than do other literatures because Yiddish literature must, above all, represent the spirit of Yiddishkayt, its inner essence. We can't spread ourselves thin like the writers of other literatures. We cannot focus on every triviality. On the contrary, we have to pack a lot of material into a small space. This also has to influence our technique. Our literature permits less "bloating" than other literatures. We have no room for flat writing.

It is the height of irony that Singer published this piece about the destruction of these cities on the day that the United States dropped an atomic bomb on Hiroshima—an event he wrote about in his next published article, "The World Will Always Remember the First Atom Bomb" (August 12, 1945). Again, as in other similar pieces, Singer juxtaposes biblical tropes with current events, using the Yiddish word-concept *khurbn*, "destruction," as his anchor. The Yiddish word is used to describe the destruction of the First and Second Temples in Jerusalem and was also used, already during World War II, as the Yiddish word for what came to be known as the Holocaust. Singer had also used the word for his 1943 story "The Destruction of Kreshev," which portrayed the moral destruction of a Jewish shtetl in preindustrial Poland. As he does in his articles on good and evil, here too Singer brings opposites together in a provocative manner, using a word associated with the destruction of Jewish life to describe the fall of Nazi Germany—suggesting that not all destructions are equal.

The Destruction of Berlin and the Destruction of Jerusalem
(August 6, 1945)

We have witnessed—almost with our own eyes—an event that is, it seems, of the greatest tragic significance. A country that set as its highest goal the annihilation of the Jews has itself been half-destroyed and completely vanquished by its enemies. Berlin is now no less destroyed than Jerusalem was when Nebuchadnezzar, the Babylonian king, besieged and conquered it. It's not clear whether the Romans did more damage to Jerusalem than the British and American bombs, as well as the Russian bullets, have done to Berlin, Hamburg, Cologne, and many other cities. Germans are now being driven out of Poland, Romania, Bulgaria, and Czechoslovakia. The Germans are now getting a taste of the destruction, persecution, expulsion, and all kinds of other things that we Jews know too well.

What's totally missing from the destruction of Germany is the tragic element. Hitler used fancy phrases. German philosophers spoke of "the dawn of the gods" and also used similar rhetorical language. But no person in their right mind feels that Germany is experiencing a tragedy in the highest sense of the word. The Germans themselves don't feel this way either. They're acting like a band of criminals who've been caught and put in jail. Like convicts who land in prison, they think, first and foremost, about eating. The first question they ask the other prisoners is: "How's the food here? How much kasha do you get? Is the soup hearty or watery? Do you get a big piece of meat or a small piece?" The Germans' second aim is to be allowed to make friends with their jailers. They want to make friends with the Americans, the English, and even the Russians as quickly as possible. Millions of young German women are ready to sell themselves. All they need are enough takers.

Those who know Jewish history know that the resistance that Jews put up against their enemies is almost as old as the Jewish nation itself. After a few hundred years of quiet a whole series of invasions began in the Land of Israel. Egypt, Assyria, Babylonia, Persia, Greece, Rome—every powerful empire of the time fought with the small, nearly unarmed people of Palestine. Every great ruler tried to force their gods, their language, and their authority onto the Jews. All of them wanted to intermix with us. Beginning with Shechem, son of Hamor, who suggested that we give them our daughters and they give us theirs, they have all proposed the same thing to us. "Why should you suffer? Why should you remain a minority, foreigners?" they argued. "Let's make a match and you'll be rid of all your troubles." . . .

Anyone who has ever been interested in the essence of tragedy knows that tragedy can only exist where there's personality. Anyone can suffer. Even an ox suffers when it's shoved or breaks a leg. But tragedy is more than simple suffering. Real tragedies represent only the suffering of the proud—those who will not surrender. Jewish fate is tragic because we have taken our burden upon ourselves. A powerful feeling of pride will not allow us to intermix with our oppressors, to efface our uniqueness.

We Jews are not racists in the sense that the word is understood today. But all Jews feel that in their blood and in their minds there is a collective spiritual and moral treasure that's a shame to lose . . .

Hitler and the German racial scientists have many times complained that the first racists were—and remain—Jews. In a certain sense, the Germans tried to imitate us. We Jews considered ourselves the "chosen" people—the Germans pronounced themselves a *herren-volk*, a master race. We had a leader, Moses, whom we called Moshe Rabbeinu. The Germans appointed their own leader. The Nazis even tried to justify their massacres and murders by saying that Jews had done the same thing. Three thousand years ago, we too eradicated the idolatrous nations of Canaan as well as the Amalekites.

The major difference between the Jewish original and the bad German copy can be best seen at its moment of failure.

We Jews have failed not once but countless times. But it was precisely these failures that lifted us up. There was no blow that could bring us to our knees. Even the latest massacres haven't fundamentally changed our way of thinking.

The loathesome German imitation is already crumbling, at the first blow. As low as they were in days of triumph, the Germans are now even lower in their days of defeat. Yesterday's "lion" is now a worm . . .

People who have enough personality to be tragic can rarely understand those whom no misfortune can render tragic. They are sentenced to decades in jail, but the only thing they think about is an extra piece of meat or how to swipe a bit of sugar or a cigarette from another prisoner. They lie in hospitals for the chronically ill, but they think only about how to pull dirty tricks on the new patients who are brought in. They are often shoved, chased, or beaten for their dirty deeds, but all they think about is petty revenge, trivial thefts, and worthless swindles. Even when they say that they regret their actions, it's nothing but a lie. They squeeze out a tear in order to arouse a little bit of sympathy from the judge. They sit in their dirty prison cells playing with cards that are falling apart, speaking coarsely, belching, hitting and insulting each other. When they're freed after many years, they go straight back to their gangs. Many go right back to committing new crimes.

Decent and sensitive people ask themselves: What's going on in the minds of people like this? Are they incapable of thinking? Don't they realize where their path leads? Don't they feel pain when they're beaten? Don't they want to be free? Have they no need of love, of family?

Many books have been written about the psychology of criminals, but for honest people they remain a mystery . . .

Criminals have their own idea of being a "chosen people," but it's a completely different kind of chosenness. It's the kind of chosenness of people who have sunk to the lowest moral level and who are proud that they can't fall any lower. They feel good at the bottom. They have nothing to fear from tomorrow. They don't have to fight for their honor. They lie in mire and spit at the sky. This is the kind of "chosen people" that the German nation has let itself become.

There are many among us who feel sorry for Germany. But the Germans themselves actually make no fuss at all about what's happened to them. Many correspondents point out that the Germans are remarkably calm. They have no regret. They're not angry at Hitler. They're not even really angry at the Allies. They run from the Russian part of Germany to the American part because they have better food . . .

The destruction of Berlin, and of Germany in general, does not represent any sort of tragedy. The Germans will adapt themselves at once to these new conditions. They'll serve anyone and plan new crimes. As much as possible, they will infect their enemies with their sickness. From time to time they'll squeeze out a tear, but its purpose will be to deceive others. For the Germans, the destruction of Berlin is just an episode . . .

This article represents another take on the question of the modern Jew, this time from the perspective of popular culture. Singer was writing the early chapters of *The Family Moskat*, reflecting on the portrayal of Jewish and Yiddish-speaking characters in American media and thinking beyond the limits of Yiddish theater and cinema—referring specifically to Paul Muni, known to Yiddish audiences as Muni Weisenfreund, who had crossed over into Hollywood. Notably, Singer makes a case for movies to take on the challenge of showing the "real" America, which includes the challenges of immigration, arguing that ignoring immigrants' stories goes against the American spirit. The article shows the forward-thinking nature of Singer's perspective on American culture as, years and decades later, these all became common themes and topics for Hollywood films.

Why Movies Aren't Made about Jewish Life

(September 23, 1945)

The five million Jews in America are, like Jews in other countries, regular moviegoers . . . So it would be natural, from time to time, for Hollywood to produce a film on a Jewish topic, just as they produce films about the Chinese, Hawaiians, Irish, French, Spanish, and Italians. What's more, Jews are a people whose life is full of conflict, dynamism, adventure. Almost every other Jew could be a character in a drama. Our lives are rich in both comedy and tragedy.

But Hollywood silences our existence. They're afraid of Jewish topics.

They use the work of mediocre amateurs. They blow events from world history out of proportion. Hollywood has made countless dramas connected with the history of Spain. Every criminal in Mexico has been "immortalized" in film. China is a beloved topic in Hollywood. This writer has already seen movies about every nation, big or small, about every social class and condition. In its own way Hollywood tries to give Americans a picture of the world, its history and problems. In the current war and earlier, when Hitler and Mussolini prepared their global massacres, Hollywood created many propaganda films that showed the evil goals and methods of the fascists, as well as the suffering of their victims. This is all well and good. But through all this Hollywood has completely omitted Jews, Jewish history, and the Jewish problem. The Nazis have in recent years exterminated six million Jews. There have been uprisings. Jews have fought alongside the partisans of other nations. But Hollywood has remained deaf and dumb. For Hollywood, we don't exist.

People who don't know that, as an industry, at least 70 or 80 percent of Hollywood lies in Jewish hands might think that Hollywood's producers, directors, and actors are one big band of antisemites. Well, we know that there's no question of antisemitism here in the normal sense of the word.

Hollywood producers are making the same mistake that Jewish assimilationists have made and are still making everywhere. They're still Jewish, but they behave almost as if they were Marranos or Anusim, afraid to reveal that they're Jewish because of the Inquisition. For them, being Jewish is a religious matter and nothing else, and since they aren't religious, or are barely religious, being Jewish is a nuisance, a handicap. Their only relationship to Judaism consists in their attempts, day and night, to clear themselves of all the conspiracies of which antisemites accuse them. When the Jew haters say that Jews are internationalists, they have to show that Jews are the most patriotic of patriots. When the antisemites say that Jews stick together and that others are like strangers to them, they have to show that they are completely alienated from their own Jewish brethren and that they actually love everyone else. Their entire existence consists in showing off for others and in keeping the heritage of our ancestors—the qualities and ideals of our people—as far away as possible.

This kind of psychology has resulted in Hollywood completely ignoring the life, the suffering, and the hopes of a great number of American citizens and a people whose past and present are both full of drama.

Hollywood does not avoid religion, as is usually the case. In England there's a ban on showing religious ceremonies in films. In the United States this is allowed. You often see Protestant ministers or Catholic priests in films. But you almost never see a rabbi. For Hollywood, greater Jewish New York does not exist—there's no colorful Lower East Side, no Jewish unions, no Jewish political parties—none of the Jewish life that represents a piece of America. Hollywood especially likes to portray people who've climbed the social ladder, immigrants who've adapted to America. But you almost never see stories about Jewish immigrants in Hollywood movies, how they came to America from small shtetls in Poland, Lithuania, or Galicia and how they worked hard here in America, raising children, going into business, and striving to establish themselves in the land of endless opportunities. We know from the newspapers that a large number of Jewish American scientists have taken part in the development of the atomic bomb. But Hollywood doesn't offer an inkling of what the children of our tailors from the old country went through before becoming American scientists, army and navy officers, prominent writers, politicians, or financiers.

Hollywood is not only sinning against Jews but also against America and the American spirit. It sins against the principles of democracy.

It's not in America's nature to renounce minorities, to ignore accomplishments, to pretend to be deaf, blind, and dumb. Americans have no reason to pretend to be ignorant or to deny their own reality. If America has several million Jews, Americans want to know who they are, where they came from, how their old country looked, how they've settled into life in their new country. Many Americans want to know how Jews are able to arrive in new places and succeed. Americans believe in success and are ready to explore and to acquaint themselves with all success stories. But Jews in Hollywood have a policy of neglecting and omitting their own kind. Hollywood has, we might think, turned being Jewish into something taboo, something banned or forbidden. Jewish actors who were raised on the Lower East Side and know Jewish life inside and out are given all sorts of roles, but never the roles that they know best: Jewish roles. Since he left Yiddish theater, it would seem that Muni Weisenfreund—known in America as Paul Muni—hasn't had even one opportunity to play a Jewish role, though it was in Jewish roles that he distinguished himself.

Hollywood never tires of offering one gangster movie after another. It turns your stomach. We constantly see the same characters speaking the same phrases. It's boring—and it offers a false picture of America. There are probably more gangster movies than gangsters. Abroad, you get the notion from Hollywood movies that America is a country that's completely infested by criminals. But at the same time they're ashamed of portraying the dramas and comedies of a noble, ancient nation.

The Hollywood assimilationists have an excuse: they

are, after all, businesspeople, and Jewish films won't interest broad audiences. But this is just an excuse . . . The truth is that there are no Jews in Hollywood who really know Jewish life. It's a desert of ignoramuses. The Jewish actors and directors in Hollywood know almost nothing about their people. They'll tell you over a glass of brandy that they are "Litvaks" or "Galitsyaners" and that their mothers light candles and recite the Shabbat blessing. But that's all they know.

In Hollywood they know how the French dressed in the fifteenth century and how Hungarians dressed in the seventeenth century. They know about all kinds of clothes and about the customs of different peoples in all different time periods. But there's no point in asking them how Jews lived in the old country or even how they live in America. And they have no inkling about Yiddish literature.

In our time, young Jewish men and women have built up the Land of Israel, revived the Hebrew language, established settlements and cities, opened factories. Jewish Palestine has had a big part in the Allied victory in the east. But for Hollywood, none of this exists.

It makes no sense to moralize against the Jews of Hollywood. They will most likely not improve much. We have simply to take the initiative ourselves. A company should be started with the express goal of producing films about Jewish life, in both Yiddish and English. Such a company would receive the support of many Jewish writers, theatrical entrepreneurs, actors, and from all of America. Not only would it be a worthy protest against Hollywood's mistreatment of Jews, it would also be a great accomplishment in its own right. Who knows? Perhaps such an undertaking may even be a financial success.

Artistically, Hollywood is heading in a bad direction. Hollywood movies are rarely logical. They're all thrown together in a hurry, without any sense, without coherence. Even if Hollywood were to make a movie about Jewish life, it would mostly likely result in a caricature . . . If, because of business, we ignore the lives of our own kind, we will end up committing many other wrongs in the name of business too. The idol of money rules everything. The box office is more important than logic, taste, or artistic integrity. Hollywood does not serve any higher purpose. There, money is the beginning and the end.

In an environment like this, Jews and their achievements can't be treated seriously. Jewish creatives have to take the burden upon themselves.

Recently, there's been a lot of talk about fighting antisemitism in America. There's no medium more suitable for the job than a good Jewish film. It certainly won't be made by Hollywood.

Among Singer's pieces on the establishment of a Jewish state, this one has been chosen as a companion to the earlier piece, "Is Being Powerless a Jewish Ideal?" (May 8, 1944), demonstrating the development of his thinking on the topic. The piece appeared three days after the first installment of *The Family Moskat*—another historical irony since the final installment, appearing just weeks before the declaration of the State of Israel, portrayed a group of Jews who had left Poland for Palestine before the outbreak of World War II, an ending that was cut from the English version of the novel. Yet the piece also reflects a question that haunts Israel over seven decades after it was established: how the democratic aspect of its founding relates to its Jewish aspect. This question is still being hotly debated and fought over today.

Answer to a Tough Question on Jewish Rights in Palestine

(November 20, 1945)

In the current conflict between Jews and England, Jews and Arabs, we sometimes hear arguments from Jews that sound very logical on the surface. This is one such argument: We all believe in democracy. We also all believe that a people inhabiting a land or territory has the right to determine its own fate. We have argued for many years that Indians should be independent in India, Chinese in China, and Albanians in Albania. So why should Arabs in Palestine, who represent a majority, not have the right to determine the fate of Palestine? How can we Jews ask that a minority prevail over a majority? How can we Jews ask that, when it comes to us, the principles for which we've all fought be changed?

This is a question that won't go away with the wave of a hand. It demands a thorough answer.

Before offering an answer, we'll relate a short anecdote. After World War I, there was a lot of crowding on the trains in Poland. It was hard to get a seat on a train car. People waited for hours on end to get on a train. Naturally, when a train came, the strongest pushed their way into the cars and took up seats. The conductors weren't able to keep better watch. It sometimes happened that the arriving passengers closed the door and didn't let anyone else board the train. One of the passengers, who had furnished himself with a comfortable seat, opened a window and looked out at the other passengers, who had pushed their way forward with their bags and were stepping on each other's feet.

A Jewish woman cried to the passenger at the window, "I beg you, have mercy, open the door!"

"The car is full," the one inside said calmly.

"So I'll stand. I have to go. It's a matter of life and death."

"My dear woman, I'm not alone in the car," answered the man. "We have all *unanimously* decided that we will not allow anyone else inside. I can't go against everyone. It was decided!"

And the poor woman was naturally left outside.

On the surface, the man was right. *Inside* the train car, the majority called for keeping the door closed. Yet this was not a true majority but an ostensible majority. The majority was *outside*, on the other side of the door. If someone had taken *their* votes into account, the decision would have been completely different.

We have a lot of such ostensible majorities in the world right now.

In Canada, ten million people have remained in their seats and almost unanimously decided that they will keep the door closed, though there is room there for many millions more. It's the majority inside a locked train car. In Australia, seven million passengers have remained seated and have almost unanimously decided that the door shouldn't be opened, though Australia is itself a whole continent. Passengers sit in all these comfortable railroad cars of the world and take only their own votes into account, not the votes of those who are standing outside banging their heads against the wall.

This is also the kind of "majority" of which the Arabs consist . . . The Arabs, like all those who have settled major territories, are in their great majority against opening the door and letting someone inside. But they also represent an ostensible democracy, not a real one. Because the real majority consists of those hundreds of millions of people who are suffocating, waiting for endless hours, years, and generations in the freezing train station, who are dying of cold and starvation. If their votes were also taken into account, the world-train would look different.

We Jews belong to this factual majority. The doors and gateways have closed on us, and when we cry out, beg, bang our heads against the wall, they tell us: The majority will not have you. You are, after all, supporters of democracy. So why can't you cope with its decisions?

Let's speak clearly. The struggle for living space is not, in essence, unjust. Nations that have been suffocated have a right to demand that they be given empty or half-empty territories.

It's true that, in the current world war, the Nazi beasts started this battle for living space. It just so happened that a group of people decided simply to invade a train car and massacre whoever was already sitting there. Then they rushed into cars where people were already packed like sardines and could barely move. Yes, in our time, the battle for living space was waged by the worst criminals in history. They have discredited this struggle, sullied it. They acted like figures from the underworld, murderers, not how those who have been wronged should act. But this is absolutely no proof that the struggle for living space is unjust in principle . . .

The struggle for a corner of one's own, for a place to lay one's head, is far from over. It's only getting started. There are hopes that the other fighters will be better people than the Germans, that they'll have a plan and an ideal. The battle is already being waged, every day, every hour. There will never be real peace on earth as long as a small group of passengers sits comfortably while the others spend the night in a cold train station. No real democracy, no *just* democracy, can even exist as long as we only count the votes of those inside rather than those outside.

If ever room is made for the outside passengers, the inside passengers will have to move over, squeeze in. Passengers who have settled into one seat, put their feet up on another, placed their hats on a third and their bags on a fourth—such passengers will have to agree to having their hats and satchels placed up on the rack. They will, naturally, make a lot of noise and say that a decision had been made in the train car and that things should remain as they were. But they will receive an answer: Outside the train car a different decision was made, and that's where the real majority lies. Yes, whole groups, whole nations, will have to move over, limit themselves a little. This is the direction of world history. Those who refuse to understand this simple truth will never understand what's happening on our little planet . . .

This writer personally believes that the world stands before a new struggle for living space—a struggle that will eclipse many old *isms* and that will change many conceptions. In the end, the progressives will be the ones who demand that the doors remain open. The reactionaries will be the ones who make every effort to keep the doors shut . . .

This piece closes the first volume both as a distilled articulation of the problem of writing Yiddish literature after the Holocaust and as an expression of creative hope. The piece exhibits the way that Singer repeatedly shifted his attention away from lamenting about issues over which he had no control, like the meager state of Yiddish readership, to issues toward which he could apply himself, like writing and publishing new material. It is easy, he says, to complain about readers, but *writers* are the real problem: they are the ones who need to develop their skills and deliver their literary goods. Most important, Singer understood that the problem, shared by readers and writers alike, was not as economic as it was spiritual. By focusing on the human spirit, he implies, writers can find ways of making their work meaningful to others—and in this way not only reach but also serve their audiences.

Increasingly Hard for Jewish Writers to Describe Jewish Life

(December 17, 1945)

On the literary scene, we speak increasingly about all kinds of problems connected with Yiddish literature. The majority complains that there are few readers. This is certainly a tragic situation. A literature can't exist without readers.

It's true that our idea of "readers" is relative. In each period, there were different ideas about *how many* readers a writer needs to have. Today it depends on each country separately. In ancient times, and even in the Middle Ages, when the number of people who could read was very small, people copied out books in a couple, or a couple dozen, copies, and they made do with this. How many readers could Shakespeare have had when the number of English people in his time was around three or four million, or even less? Anyway, most English people couldn't read or were not interested in literature. How many readers do contemporary Finnish, Czech, Bulgarian, Serbian, Hungarian, Lithuanian, or even Norwegian and Danish writers have if they aren't translated into other languages? Yet writers exist in all these nations.

So the number of readers that writers need is not ascertainable. Whatever they have, that's what they've got. It depends on a thousand factors. We also know that the number of readers that writers have in no way determines the writers' value. What we'd like to suggest is that the problem of readers is a very important one for Yiddish literature, but it's not the only problem.

We'd like to point to a problem here that is, in our opinion, just as important as the problem of readers, and maybe even more important. It's the problem of *writers*.

The fact that our old home has been destroyed and that Yiddish writers have been sitting in America for decades, cut off from the sources of Jewish life and from the Yiddish language, has often had a bad influence on them. We slowly forget Yiddish and, chiefly, the Jewish way of life that was so rich in customs. Forgetting is human. Cut a rabbi off from his religious books for thirty or forty years, and he'll start making foolish mistakes. He'll remember many things very well, but he'll forget others. He'll be half scholar and half ignoramus. He'll remember a difficult part of the Tosafot, but he'll forget a section of the Torah or he'll confuse one part with the other. America is full of such half scholars. Time has taken its toll. Naturally, we are speaking here of scholars who have stopped studying.

Something similar is happening to those who have long been cut off from the Yiddish language. If they remember a thousand things, they also forget a thousand. Let them read a book by Sholem Aleichem or by Y. L. Peretz and they say, "Hey, I've forgotten these words and expressions." And they themselves can't believe that this is possible.

Time takes its toll, but we Yiddish writers do very little to resist the power of forgetting.

Simplistic thinking says that, for Yiddish literature to exist, we need to record every word, every expression, every custom, every single aspect of our way of life. Simplistic thinking dictates that Yiddish writers should spend a lot of time and even money on remembrance—on immortalizing the way of life and the language of our mothers and fathers. But this is not being done, or else it's being done carelessly and by a small number of writers. A strange process has taken place for some writers: their language has been watered down. It's no longer their mother tongue. The sap has dried out. This in no way implies that these writers have lost their talent. They've simply forgotten the language and its usage little by little.

You read such writers and think: What language are they speaking? Ostensibly it's Yiddish, and yet this is not Yiddish. They portray characters, they make them speak, but they don't talk like Jews used to talk. You sometimes read a poem or a play, and you have the same feeling, over and over, that it smacks of uprootedness. It's as if someone who's not Jewish had learned Yiddish.

It's true that here in America there's a new Jewish life and a new Jewish lifestyle. But a majority of Yiddish writers have not yet digested this new way of life, not yet found its linguistic medium. It's a big question whether Yiddish will one day be able to portray this new version of Jewish life. In the meantime the old version is being forgotten by both readers and writers.

If a miracle takes place and a Jewish millionaire establishes a major publishing house, creating an apparatus to distribute Yiddish books throughout the entire world, Yiddish literature will still be far from solving its problem. There will still be the big question of content.

A great number of readers who answered our survey about why newspaper readers read no Yiddish books replied that many books that they've been sold aren't Yiddish. Some sound like they've been translated from English. Others are simply bland. Others still are written in such a way that they can't tell what the writers had in mind. They say things, they call things out, they warn against things, but you don't know what they want. You can't understand what they say because they literally sound crazy. You try to understand it as a symbol, an allegory, but you can't figure out what it symbolizes.

The Dubner Magid and other traveling preachers also used allegories, but people with a good head on their shoulders were able to grasp what they were getting at. Some modern works are written in such a way that, no matter how smart you are, no matter how sharp your sense for allusions and hints, you still can't understand their meaning, and it becomes strangely tedious. The words aren't rooted in Jewish life and the Jewish spirit. They are simply words taken from the dictionary.

There's no one more profound than Baruch Spinoza, whose *Ethics* is written in an extremely short manner, very condensed. A single one of his sentences often says more than an entire volume written by another philosopher. Few scholars have reached the greatest depths of his teaching. But his words ring like pure crystal and are remarkably clear. It's like looking into a deep body of water. It's the depth that refreshes you, even if you can't get to the bottom of it. It's a depth with a foundation in life, in the mind . . .

Our parents and grandparents studied Judaism their whole lives. We, their children, do not. We've convinced ourselves that Judaism is a Torah—a teaching—that we learn once and then have enough of forever. This is absolutely false.

If this writer had the time and money he would establish a study house, or a yeshiva, for Yiddish writers. It would store Yiddish books and Hebrew books and books about Judaism in other languages. People would take lessons there about the Yiddish language and about Jewish life and customs—about Jewish history and Jewish spiritual tendencies. It's not enough for a writer to have gone to heder until the age of eleven. Yiddish writers have to go to heder for their whole lives. Yiddish writers have to be learned Torah scholars, in the old sense of the word and also in a new sense. If not, there will be a spiritual catastrophe . . .

Like most problems, the problem of Yiddish literature possesses a spiritual character. It's a crisis that's far less economic than spiritual . . . Yiddish writers have to study if they want there to be a Yiddish literature.

Acknowledgments

This edited and translated volume is the result of over ten years of focused interest in the writings of Isaac Bashevis Singer. It is closer, in many ways, to the collection I had originally intended to produce in 2013, when, setting out to explore Singer's essayistic writings, I found a trove of English-language essays at the Harry Ransom Center, Austin, most of which were translated or revised directly by him. Before I could set upon translating and editing new work, I felt, I had first to bring his own own efforts to light. Once that book, *Old Truths and New Clichés*, finally appeared, in 2022, it became possible to pursue the publication of previously untranslated material—introducing a new phase in bringing out some of the writings still largely relegated to the microfilmed pages of the Yiddish daily *Forverts*.

My own personal life has changed greatly throughout the ten years since I first began compiling the list of articles that would eventually become this volume. I met my wife, Aleza, in 2015, and in the next seven years we brought three girls into the world, Kedem Sarai, Alma Zisel, and Sinai Ruth. The four of them are, in many ways, the ones who deserve my gratitude in preparing and publishing this volume—since they all, in different ways, had to tolerate the hours, days, months, and years that it took to turn a spreadsheet of potential articles into an actual book that can be read by others.

Professionally, too, I owe considerable thanks to people who have helped me retain my commitment to translating and publishing Singer's work. At the top of the list is Susan Schulman, agent of the Singer Literary Trust, who has mentored me in the ways of publishing and made it possible for me to pursue a decade of literary production—which I can only hope continues. In addition, I owe thanks to all of Singer's grandchildren, who have not only entrusted me with the task of advising them on their mission to maintain Singer's literary legacy but who have committed to developing that legacy with new material. It is a testament to the vision of Singer's son, Israel Zamir (1929–2014), that they work together as a family unit to honor the memory of their father and grandfather.

Everyone needs to be advised, including those who advise others, and for both their advice and support I deeply thank David Roskies, Leona Toker, Peter Cole, Adina Hoffman, Eli Lederhendler, Ruth Fine, Menahem Blondheim, Uzi Rebhun, Shuli Barzilai, Val Vinokur, Ofer Dynes, Magda Teter, Eddy Portnoy, Boris Dralyuk, Gail Hareven, Amnon Ben-Ami, Alon Levitan, Velina Minkoff, Annie Kantar Ben-Hillel, and Gilad Jacobson. I am also grateful to the fellow translators with whom I have worked on a variety of projects—especially Daniel Kennedy, Ri J. Turner, and Shiri Shapira—whose collective integrity and dedication to Yiddish and to translation are like beacons in a turbulent sea of literary survival.

Finally, everyone at the Yiddish Book Center and White Goat Press deserves considerable kudos for providing the support and infrastructure to translate, edit, and publish this book. I want particularly to thank Aaron Lansky and Lisa Newman, who believed in the project before reading a single word, as well as their colleagues, all of whom have devoted their professional lives to the cause of Yiddish. I am especially indebted to Yankl Salant, translation editor of this volume, whose edits and comments turned into a fruitful dialogue that greatly enriched its pages. Without these people, and many others working behind the scenes, this volume would still be a spreadsheet on my hard drive, waiting to be turned into a book.

Isaac Bashevis Singer (1903–1991) was a Polish-born Jewish-American author of novels, short stories, memoirs, essays, and stories for children. His career spanned nearly seven decades of literary production, much of it spent translating his own work from Yiddish into English, which he undertook with various collaborators and editors. Singer published widely during his lifetime, with nearly sixty stories appearing in *The New Yorker*, and received numerous awards and prizes, including two Newbery Honor Book Awards (1968 and 1969), two National Book Awards (1970 and 1974), and the Nobel Prize for Literature (1978). Known for fiction that portrayed 19th-century Polish Jewry as well as supernatural tales that combined Jewish mysticism with demonology, Singer was a master storyteller whose sights were set squarely on the tension between human nature and the human spirit.

David Stromberg is a writer, translator, and literary scholar. His work has appeared in *The American Scholar*, *Woven Tale Press*, and the *Los Angeles Review of Books*, among others. In his role as editor of the Isaac Bashevis Singer Literary Trust he has published *Old Truths and New Clichés* (Princeton University Press), a collection of Singer's essays, and a new translation of the canonical story *Simple Gimpl: The Definitive Bilingual Edition* (Restless Books). Among Stromberg's recent writing is a series of speculative essays, including "A Short Inquiry into the End of the World" (*The Massachusetts Review*), "The Eternal Hope of the Wandering Jew" (*The Hedgehog Review*), and "To Kill an Intellectual" (*The Fortnightly Review*). He is based in Jerusalem.

About White Goat Press

White Goat Press, the Yiddish Book Center's imprint, is committed to bringing newly translated work to the widest readership possible. We publish work in all genres—novels, short stories, drama, poetry, memoirs, essays, reportage, children's literature, plays, and popular fiction, including romance and detective stories.

whitegoatpress.org
The Yiddish Book Center's imprint